POWER GENERATION
THE ROUTE TO OPERATING SUCCESS

POWER GENERATION
THE ROUTE TO OPERATING SUCCESS

The Second International Conference
sponsored by
The Institution of Diesel and Gas Turbine Engineers
and held at
The City Conference Centre, Mark Lane, London
on
16 March 1989

Published by
Mechanical Engineering Publications Limited for
The Institution of Diesel and Gas Turbine Engineers
LONDON

The Publishers are not responsible for any statement made in this publication. Data, discussion and conclusions developed by authors are for information only and are not intended for use without independent substantiating investigation on the part of potential users.

Printed by Waveney Print Services Ltd, Beccles, Suffolk

CONTENTS

INTRODUCTION

Welcome to the second international conference sponsored by the Institution of Diesel and Gas Turbine Engineers.

This conference is a major item in our seventy-fifth anniversary year. It covers the principal issues affecting the generation of electrical power using diesel and gas turbine prime movers. The programme is purposely wide-ranging and reflects the multi-disciplinary skills needed to successfully generate power for an individual user, an industrial complex, or a local utility.

Authors of the individual papers are from major manufacturers, consultants, and users in the United Kingdom and overseas. The Institution is grateful for their commitment, and I would like to add my personal thanks to the authors for meeting the sometimes tight deadlines.

I hope you enjoy the conference.

Graham Dilliway

J. G. DILLIWAY

The technical and financial analysis of prime movers

P M EMMS, BSc, CEng, MIMechE
Senior Mechanical and Electrical Engineer, Property Services Agency

Biographical Notes

Paul Emms is a senior mechanical and electrical engineer with the Property Services Agency (PSA), which is responsible for the design, construction and maintenance of much of the British Government's civil and military estate in the UK and overseas. He has been with the PSA for 18 years and has been associated with the design and development of electrical power systems for the Agency, and is currently project manager for the construction of a 16 megawatt diesel engined generating station in Scotland.

Synopsis

The 3 common prime movers used in industrial power systems are diesel engines, gas turbines and steam turbines. The range in capacity of these units generally gives the engineer a choice in meeting the requirements for supplying electricity. This paper looks at each of the common prime movers and the parameters that may make one more suitable than any other.

Where a particular project does have a number of technically acceptable solutions, the paper goes on to describe the typical criteria an engineer must consider in economic analysis in order to determine the most appropriate economic solution.

1.00 INTRODUCTION

1.01 Engineers today are faced not only with engineering a successful system that meets the requirement to supply electricity of the right quality but also to ensure the system is the most economic.

1.02 Prime movers currently available often give the engineer a choice of types that are technically suitable but the available options must be evaluated economically to demonstrate value for money and justify the investment.

1.03 This paper describes the 3 common prime movers used for generating electricity and describes the parameters that can make one system more suitable for a particular application than another. Where there is more than one technical solution that meets the requirements, the paper guides the engineer in evaluating the economics to determine the most appropriate system.

2.00 PRIME MOVERS

Three basic types of prime mover are found in industrial power systems, diesel engines, gas and steam turbines. They all have specific operating parameters which effect their suitability for an industrial power system. The most flexible in terms of operation and electrical generating efficiency is the diesel engine and consequently are found in industrial power systems throughout the world.

2.01 DIESEL ENGINE

Diesel generating sets are available in unit sizes from 5 kW, using high speed automotive type engines to more than 24 MW, using slow speed large bore marine types. Consequently they are used as prime movers in the largest industrial power systems, with multiple units operating in parallel. Diesel alternator generating sets have an electrical efficiency of about 38% and are used when the electrical supply requirement is the only or predominant load requirement.

The amount of energy released during the combustion process in a diesel engine of a particular size can be increased if more fuel can be burned, but that is dictated by the amount of air available. The amount of air can be increased by pressurising the combustion air using an exhaust gas driven air compressor (turbocharger) and cooling the air using an intercooler, output can be increased by as much as 3 times. Turbo chargers may also be used to counteract the effects of altitude and temperature at the generating plant site. The output of a naturally aspirated engine will fall by approximately 1% for every 100 metre increase in altitude and also by about 3% for every 10 deg C. increase in ambient temperature above ISO reference conditions (15 deg C. and 760 Tor), see figures 1 and 2.

2.02 Diesel engines can be part of a combined heat and power system with heat recovered from engine exhaust gases, cooling water, lubricating oil and combustion air. About 60% of the energy released when fuel is burnt is converted to thermal rather than mechanical energy, see fig 3. The heat recovered from the exhaust gases can provide hot water or steam at about 300 deg C, but heat recovered from the various cooling systems will give only low grade energy; typically hot water at about 60 deg C. This can be used for local space heating, domestic hot water or feed water heating, see fig 4 showing a typical schematic.

2.03 There is a vast number of wearing components in a diesel engine and consequently the maintenance burden is high, virtually all components require some maintenance at varying intervals. Consequently, non-stop running of a diesel engine must be limited to periods of about 1000 hours duration before inspection, adjustment and maintenance is required. Where a non-stop supply of electricity is required this constraint poses difficulty. Continuous generation of electricity from diesel plant can only be reliably achieved by the installation of several generating sets, each rated at a fraction of the maximum demand, with the total number of sets being at least 2 more than is necessary to meet the maximum demand. This allows plant to be held in reserve for maintenance and occasional breakdowns of running sets.

2.04 Diesel generating sets are capable of providing an electrical supply between 5 and 30 seconds from start initiation, depending on size and state of readiness. The ability of a diesel generating set to accept sudden load changes is generally limited by its combustion air system.

Typically a naturally aspirated engine can accept its full rated load in one step whereas if turbo charged only 70%, and if turbo charged and inter cooled only 50%.

2.05 The voltage and freqency disturbances from steady state conditions when loads are applied are related to the reactance of the alternator and momentum of rotating parts respectively, the automatic voltage regulator and governer restoring voltage and frequency to steady state values. As a guide, Table 1 shows the voltage and frequency disturbances which can be expected.

3.00 GAS TURBINE

3.01 Where there is a requirement for long periods of non stop operation, the gas turbine is an effective prime mover. Gas turbines are available from around 500 kW to about 70 MW but compared with diesel engines are not available in many sizes, particularly below 10 MW and therefore cannot be exactly tailored to the users likely power demand.

3.02 The largest outlet for gas turbines, is of course, in aero engine applications and many electrical power plant gas turbines are based on units developed for use in aircraft. Other gas turbines have now been developed specifically for use in electrical power generating applications.

3.03 Gas turbines have an efficiency below 30%, typically 25% and can be as low as 15% for a small gas turbine (500 kW). They are particularly sensitive to operating conditions, especially ambient temperature, and their rated output reduces by 1% per deg C. and 1% per 100 m above standard ISO conditions (15 deg C. and 760 Tor, see figures 1 and 2).

3.04 Excess air in a gas turbine combustion system will allow auxilliary firing of the exhaust gas. Heat can be recovered from the exhaust gas if required or an auxilliary boiler may be used to increase the exhaust gas energy for a specific purpose, see Figure 5. The exhaust gas may be used directly in an industrial drying process if air quality is not important, obviously avoiding energy loss from heat exchange systems.

3.05 The ability of a gas turbine to accept step loads is dependent on whether the machine is a single or 2 shaft type, see Figures 6 and 7. The single shaft turbine has the gas generator and power turbine directly coupled. The electrical generator connected through a gear box since shaft speed is greater than that required for power generation purposes. Having a high angular momentum and constant combustion airflow irrespective of the electrical load means a single shaft gas turbine has to accommodate load changes by a change in fuelling rate only. A 2 shaft machine has the turbine separated into 2 mechanically independent parts, a high pressure turbine and a low pressure turbine. The high pressure turbine is on the same shaft as the compressor and provides the power to drive it. The low pressure turbine provides the power to drive the electrical generator and since it is not coupled mechanically to the high pressure turbine it can rotate at a different speed. The advantage of a free power turbine system are that it is possible to avoid the use of a speed reduction gearbox and the speed of the gas generator can be altered independently according to the load demand. The airflow through the gas generator and power turbine is broadly proportional to the electrical load and load changes are accommodated by a change in both airflow and fuelling rate.

3.06 The single shaft machine can usually accept full rated load in one step with only a 2% deviation in frequency and therefore has excellent step load frequency response. As a guide, Table 2 shows voltage and frequency disturbances which can be expected from a single shaft gas turbine.

3.07 Before a gas turbine can produce power it is necessary to run the compressor up to a speed sufficient to provide adequate air to the combustion chamber. It is therefore unlikely that a gas turbine would be used as a prime mover for a standby supply unless the system can accommodate a period of at least 1 minute from start initiation to electricity supply available.

4.00 STEAM TURBINE

4.01 The steam turbine, provided water treatment and steam conditions are properly controlled, is the most maintenance free prime mover. They are available in sizes from about 1 MW to units in access of 1500 MW. Consequently steam turbines are of most use in a large-scale power system where long periods of operation are necessary, typically a utility system where steam is available or is required for an industrial process.

4.02 In the case of a straight condensing turbine, see Figure 8, the entire steam pressure drop is utilised and efficiencies in the order of 40% are obtainable, with the remainder of the energy transferred to the condenser cooling medium. Whilst the steam turbine is a much smaller prime mover than either the gas turbine or diesel engine for the same unit output, the auxilliary equipment takes up very much more space. A great advantage with the steam turbine is that the steam raising plant can be designed to accommodate a wide range of fuels so taking advantage of market prices.

4.03 Steam turbines are not as flexible as either the single shaft gas turbine or diesel engines when accommodating changes in electrical load and consequently they are generally used where the system capacity is very much larger than the largest step load on the system.

5.00 ECONOMIC ANALYSES

5.01 With the wide range of equipment that is available there is seldom any doubts that the technical requirements of a system cannot be met. Many companies are now investing large sums of money in generating plant and it is essential to ensure value for money and justify the investment. Economic analyses must demonstrate that capital invested will be recovered during the life of the plant and that the type of generating plant proposed is the most economic.

5.02 An economic analysis which considers expenditure not in just capital terms but also the operating life is the discounted cash flow technique. This enables a net present value to be calculated for each particular scheme and comparisons to be made. The net present value being a representation of future costs and benefits at a present day cost. Obviously the accuracy of any economic analysis is only as good as the accuracy of the estimates that form part of it.

5.03 The effect of a change in any one element of the economic analysis can be assessed by sensitivity tests. The cost of fuel tends to vary unpredictably so any estimates of fuel costs can be tested to assess the effect on the net present value. Typically net present values can be calculated using fuel costs 10% higher and 10% lower for each available option to see if the most economic solution changes. These recalculations highlight any condition when the initial optimum solution could be overtaken by another competing solution. The likelihood of the alternative solution occurring can be assessed and a decision made. It is appreciated that fuel costs do vary by more than 10% but in general terms, the relationship between different energy sources remains reasonably constant.

5.04 Various technical solutions must be identified in a logical manner. The first option is probably to consider increasing the reliability of the incoming utility supply, if one exists. It may be possible to obtain a dual independent utility supply and consequently the incidence of supply failure will be extremely low but still vulnerable to massive grid failures and industrial action. Installation costs will be substantially greater than a single utility supply but nevertheless the net present value of this option can be calculated and compared with others.

5.05 Private generating plant sized to meet the load requirements will be an option, but additional units to those necessary to meet the maximum demand will be needed for maintenance and breakdown. Consideration should be given to load shedding when the incoming utility is interrupted since this will reduce the capacity of generating plant required and improve economics. Total independence may only be economic where abundant cheap fuel is available or there is a well matched requirement for process heat. Although private generation will not be affected by disruption to the utility supply there is the possibility that industrial action could spread to the personnel operating the private plant or to the delivery of essential supplies.

5.06 The type of prime mover is important in an economic analysis. High speed diesel engines generally use relatively expensive light fuel oils but are cheaper than low speed engines of the same output, using comparatively cheap residual fuels. Capital cost of gas turbine plant is often more expensive than diesel equipment, but may be cheaper overall. The relatively low cost of effective silencing, the lightweight and consequent low civil costs and the absence of cooling requirements should be taken into account when calculating the net present value of this option. Similarly the apparent high capital costs of steam turbine plant has to be considered in the light of process steam availability. A boiler may be capable of producing more steam than is required for an industrial process and could be used for electrical generation purposes. In a town centre where space is scarce standby sets which can be accommodated easily is an important feature. The cost of the space occupied by the generating plant is often ignored, particularly if the land is not currently required for any other purpose. The cost of land should be included in an economic appraisal as it may be required for development at a later date or for sale or lease.

5.07 Operating costs are important, fuel costs are generally less important for standby systems than capital cost, while the reverse is true for base load systems. Standby systems will be used infrequently and the overall fuel consumption is therefore low but the cost of fuel storage and the initial fuel stock is considerable. Standby systems operating from natural gas do not have fuel storage problems but the gas supply authority may impose substantial charges, particularly if the standby set represents the principle gas load on the site.

5.08 Although standby sets are operated infrequently it is necessary to make allowance for inspection, maintenance and testing in addition to any staffing costs during periods of operation. It is of great importance that equipment suppliers maintenance instructions are followed. Failure to perform adequate servicing is the prime cause of plant malfunction in standby equipment.

5.09 The installation of on-site generating plant may increase the operators liability to local authority rates particularly if new buildings are erected to house the plant. Extra insurance may also be required to cover the plant itself.

5.10 The economic analyses must be developed logically. Table 3 shows a typical power system option table establishing a bottom line, like for like, comparison to be made.

6.00 CONCLUSION

6.01 The 3 prime mover types commonly used for generating plant each have particular advantages and disadvantages. The ranges of capacity in which these prime movers can be obtained generally means an engineer has a choice to make for a particular scheme being considered.

6.02 It is important to examine all the options available and use an investment appraisal technique at an early stage in order to optimise expenditure over the years. The choice of generating plant has to be carefully planned and economically assessed so that the most appropriate economic solution can be determined.

ACKNOWLEDGMENTS

The author wishes to record his thanks to the Property Services Agency for permission to present this paper and to his friends and colleagues for assistance in its preparation. The views expressed are those of the author and do not necessarily coincide with those of the Property Services Agency.

BIBLIOGRAPHY

(i) Industrial Power Systems - IEE Conference J G Dilliway December 1986

(ii) Electric Power Plant International- The Electrical Research Association Ltd.

TABLE 1

	Steady State	25% load step (back to steady state limits in 1 second)
Voltage	+ − 0.5%	+ − 2.5%
		25% load step (back to steady state limits in 2 seconds)
Frequency	+ − 0.5%	+ − 2.0%

Table 2

	Steady State	25% load step (back to steady state conditions in 1 second)
Voltage	+ − 0.5%	+ − 2.5%

		25% load step (back to steady state conditions in 2 seconds)
Frequency	+ − 0.5%	+ − 1.0%

TABLE 3

Typical power system table

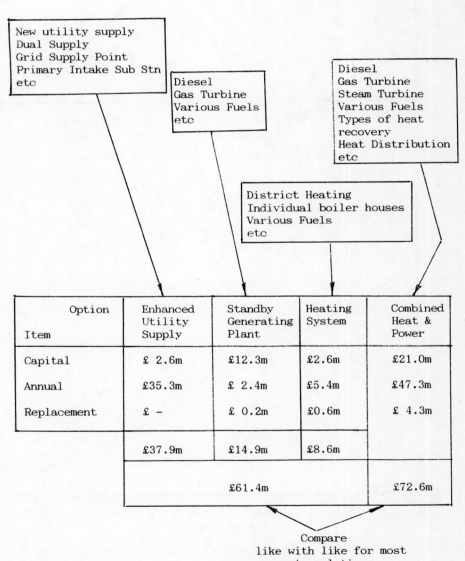

Option Item	Enhanced Utility Supply	Standby Generating Plant	Heating System	Combined Heat & Power
Capital	£ 2.6m	£12.3m	£2.6m	£21.0m
Annual	£35.3m	£ 2.4m	£5.4m	£47.3m
Replacement	£ –	£ 0.2m	£0.6m	£ 4.3m
	£37.9m	£14.9m	£8.6m	
		£61.4m		£72.6m

Compare
like with like for most
economic solution

Boxes (inputs to table):

New utility supply
Dual Supply
Grid Supply Point
Primary Intake Sub Stn
etc

Diesel
Gas Turbine
Various Fuels
etc

Diesel
Gas Turbine
Steam Turbine
Various Fuels
Types of heat recovery
Heat Distribution
etc

District Heating
Individual boiler houses
Various Fuels
etc

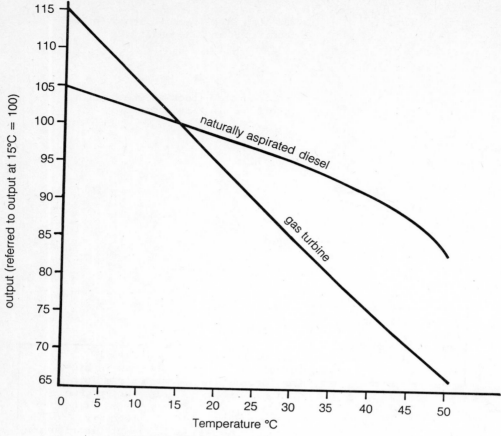

Fig 1   Typical variation of output with temperature

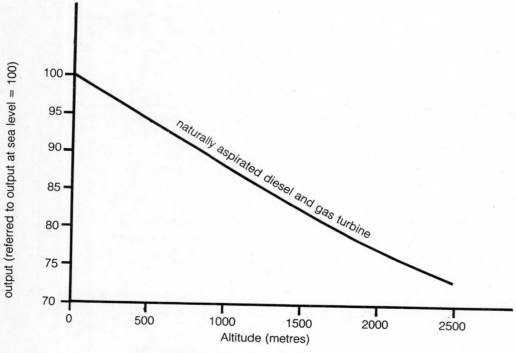

Fig 2   Typical variation of output with altitude

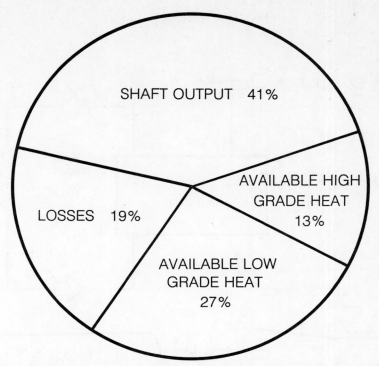

Fig 3   Heat balance for diesel engines fitted with heat recovery equipment

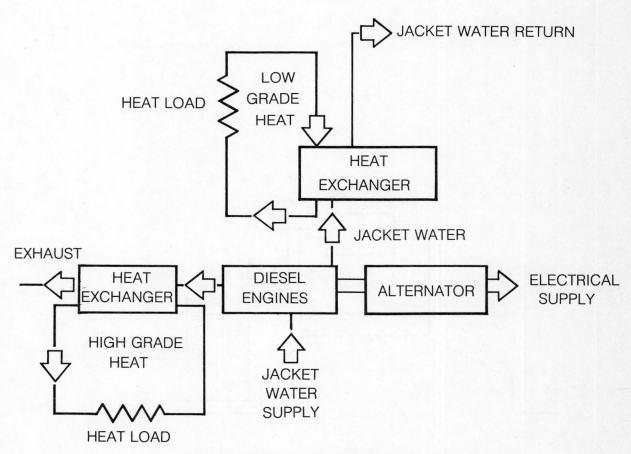

Fig 4   CHP system utilising diesel engines

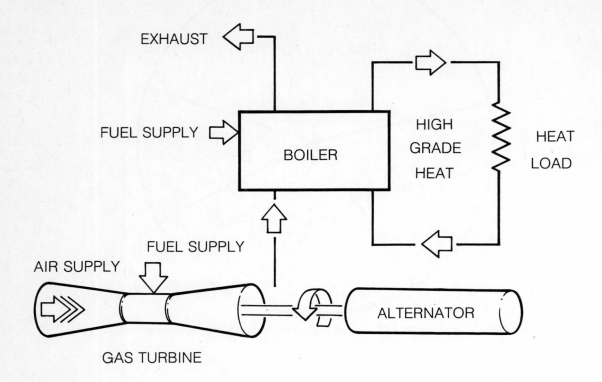

Fig 5   Simple CHP system utilising gas turbines and auxiliary boiler

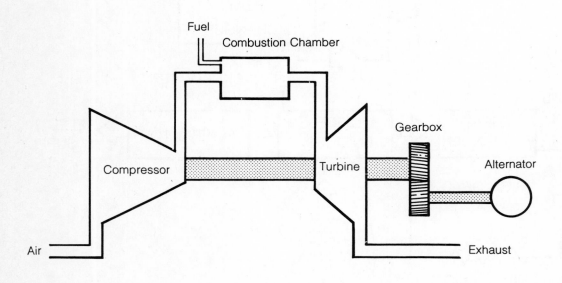

Fig 6   Single shaft gas turbine

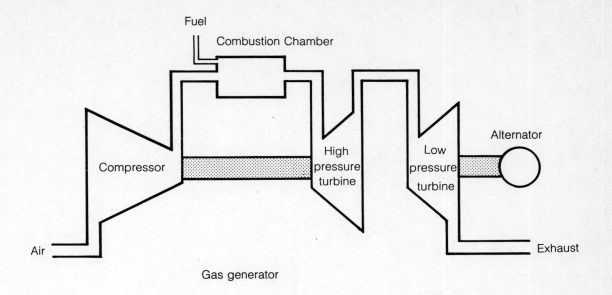

Gas generator

Fig 7   Two-shaft gas turbine

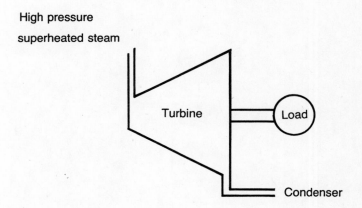

Fig 8   Straight condensing turbine

Fuel selection and management

C FISHER, AMIMarE, FInstDiagE, MInstPet
Director of Marketing, Veritas Petroleum Services Limited

Introduction

In this paper, the writer has attempted to highlight some of the fuel related problems which have been experienced by operators of low and medium speed diesel engines.

Worldwide fuel quality statistics have been produced from the unique VPS data base and these are used to demonstrate the different fuel qualities generally available around the world today. The main reasons for these quality variations are considered together with average distillate and heavy fuel prices.

In particular, emphasis has been placed upon the importance of fuel analysis if efficient and correct fuel treatment and engine operation are to be achieved.

The main fuel quality parameters and their significance are reviewed in conjunction with potential machinery problems.

Some case histories from the VPS records illustrate the problems which have been encountered by Shipowners during the last decade.

The writer considers that whether the power plant is based ashore or at sea, the problems which may be experienced as a result of using fuel of uncertain quality are identical.

BACK GROUND

Shipowners began to change from coal to oil for firing boilers early in the 1900's. The second quarter of this Century saw development of diesel engines for marine propulsion and right up to the late 1970's fuel quality had not been a major problem.

The Gulf War in the 1970's produced a threefold rise in the price of fuel oil and improvements in refinery methods resulted in dramatic changes to the quality of marine residual fuels.

These problems are not restricted to ocean going vessels but will affect the costs and maintenance management of any industry which uses liquid fuel in boilers and engines.

Veritas Petroleum Services analyse some 15000 fuel samples a year, submitted by Chief Engineers of ocean going vessels trading worldwide. Veritas provide these engineers with a detailed analysis telex report including technical advice regarding fuel treatment and expected engine performance.

A data base has now been established which records all the analysis results over the last 6 years. This data may be extracted by country, port, fuel supplier, grade or by individual parameters of fuel quality.

GEOGRAPHICAL QUALITY VARIANCE

Tables 1, 2 and 3 have been compiled using this data base to highlight geographical differences in fuel oil quality.

The grade and quality of fuels available in each part of the world is governed by several variables such as:-

* Local crude oil source and quality

* Local refining techniques which are developed to meet demands for particular end products.

* Quality and origin of imported crude or fuels

* Blending techniques

* Refinery and distribution housekeeping

* Level of activity of major suppliers

* Demand

The local crude oil quality or the quality of imported crude combined with the refining technique will be largely responsible for the quality of residue after the extraction of lighter products. It should be remembered that heavy fuel oil is a refinery by product which is produced from blends of residues and distillates. The prime function of the refinery being to maximise the yields of more valuable lighter distillates from the crude oil.

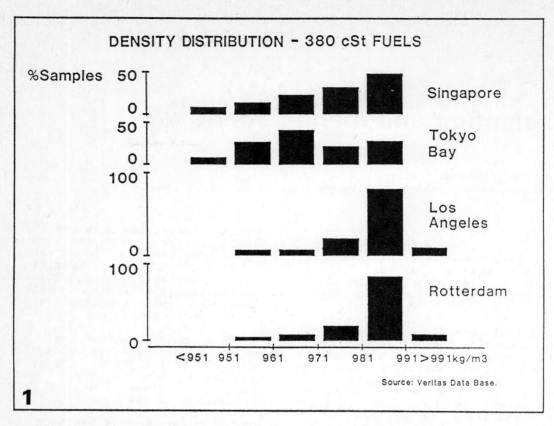

DENSITY DISTRIBUTION - 380 cSt FUELS

%Samples

Singapore

Tokyo Bay

Los Angeles

Rotterdam

<951 951 961 971 981 991 >991kg/m3

Source: Veritas Data Base.

1

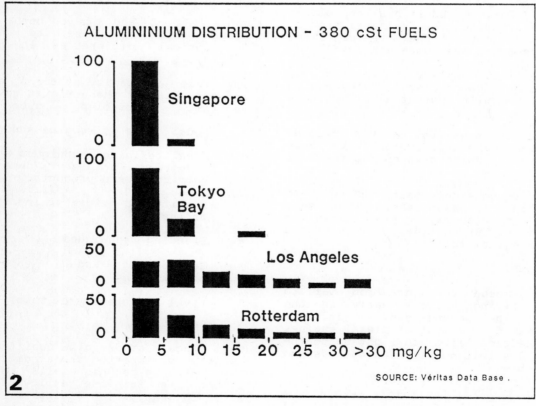

ALUMININIUM DISTRIBUTION - 380 cSt FUELS

Singapore

Tokyo Bay

Los Angeles

Rotterdam

0   5   10   15   20   25   30 >30 mg/kg

SOURCE: Véritas Data Base .

2

Frankly, the heavy fuel oil purchased today is what is left after the valuable elements of the original crude have been extracted.

Singapore fuels tend to have higher carbon residue and negligible aluminium contents. This reflects the lack of catalytic cracking in this region. Los Angeles fuels, where extensive catalytic cracking is conducted, show higher levels of aluminium and density but lower levels of carbon residue. This information helps the fuel user to understand why fuels purchased in various parts of the world will vary in quality and to be aware of potential problems.

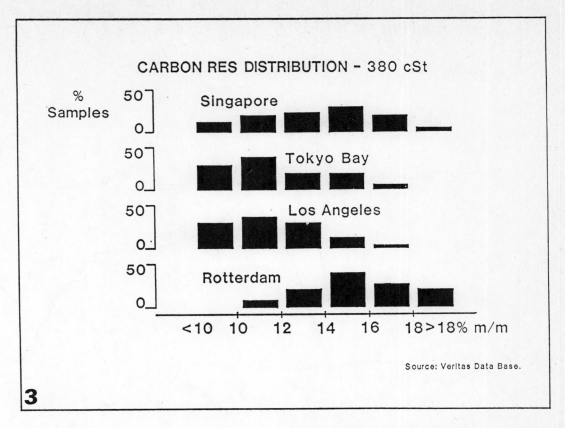

CARBON RES DISTRIBUTION - 380 cSt

Source: Veritas Data Base.

3

Fuel Prices.

Fuel prices will continue to fluctuate as a result of political influences, market forces and technological advances. It could be argued that market forces eventually correct political disturbances but the problem remains that predicting these upsets is almost impossible.

The purchaser should be able to save money by understanding the fuel market and obtaining best prices for a particular fuel quality. In addition, he has the choice of using high or low grade fuels.

Again the Veritas Statistics will prove useful during purchasing negotiations and grade selection. Our analysis statistics indicate that there is no guarantee that a higher grade fuel oil (lower viscosity) will be of overall superior quality to a lower grade fuel (high viscosity) oil on all deliveries.

In addition, by comparing specific energies of fuels in different grades against costs, the user will be in a better position to evaluate the savings in changing from one grade to another.

It can be seen from Table 4 that there have been dramatic changes in the cost of both heavy fuel and diesel oil since 1973.

In 1973 HFO was selling at some 38 USD per metric ton with diesel oil around 70 USD/ton. By 1980, the HFO had escalated to 215 USD/ton whilst diesel oil peaked in 1979 to over 300 USD/ton. Over the years it would seem safe to say that diesel oil purchasers would have been paying twice as much for their fuel as those using heavy fuel.

Perhaps we should look at this over a year with a plant consuming say 150 tons of fuel a day.

Fuel Bill for the Year - 1988

HFO	D.O.
(150 x 366 x 50)	(150 x 366 x 110)
2.745 Million USD	6.039 Million USD

We should of course allow for the difference in heating value of the two fuels. Specific energy approximation for HFO would be around 40 MJ/kg whereas an average for a diesel oil would be approximately 42 MJ/kg. Therefore, we should add approximately 5% to the cost of the HFO to achieve an equivalent energy cost. This would still give a price differential of some 3 million USD.

Obviously, we would then need to consider the additional costs of heating and treating the HFO.

This type of calculation would be made at the design stage of a power plant, however, decisions are often made later during operation to change from using heavy fuel oil to distillate, due to the high maintenance costs associated with HFO operation.

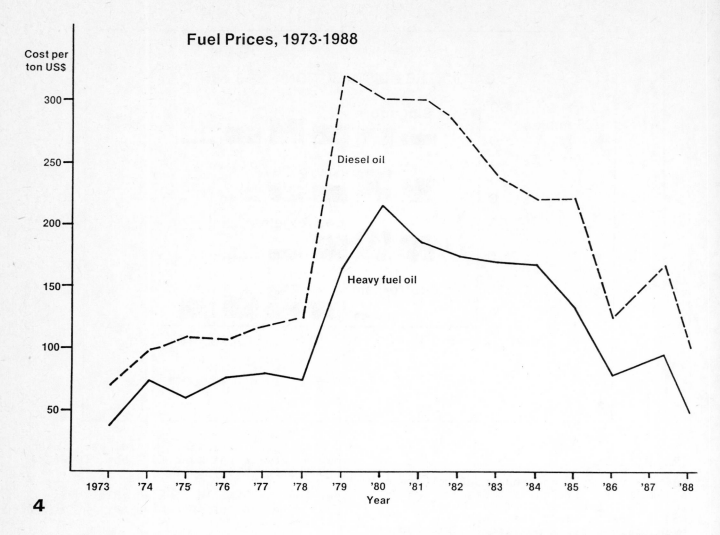

Fuel Prices, 1973-1988

Cost per ton US$

Diesel oil

Heavy fuel oil

1973 '74 '75 '76 '77 '78 '79 '80 '81 '82 '83 '84 '85 '86 '87 '88

Year

4

In this paper, the writer has attempted to identify the problems associated with using lower quality fuels and demonstrate the importance of fuel quality analysis as an essential part of the fuel treatment process. High levels of maintenance and reduced machinery availability should not automatically be associated with poor quality fuel but perhaps more directly to a limited understanding of the effects of inadequately treating fuels prior to burning.

Whether the fuel user is a Chief Engineer of a Ship or a Power Station, his prime objectives must be to optimise machinery availability, minimise downtime periods and run an efficient plant with minimal maintenance costs.

Of course, the selection of machinery is most important but a second key factor is that of fuel quality.

The design engineers hopefully will provide a complete fuel treatment plant which will be able to successfully treat the type of fuel which is not only suitable for the engine but also capable of dealing with the quality of fuel generally available in the area. On first sight, it may appear to be easier to arrange for a shore installation rather than a ship which trades in all

ports of the world. However, with new refinery techniques being introduced in all parts of the world it cannot be assumed that an historically good fuel quality area will remain so.

Selecting a Fuel to suit a Particular Power Plant

The economics of using a high grade fuel as opposed to a low grade fuel will need to be frequently reviewed.

The price differential will be one factor but the following points must be evaluated when considering the overall costs of using low grade fuels.

1) Additional treatment costs
   a) Heating during storage
   b) Purification
   c) Filtration
   d) Heating for injection
   e) Maintenance of treatment plant
      – parts and labour.

2) Potential increase in fuel related engine problems.

3) Potential increase in maintenance, manpower and spares.

4) Potential reduction in plant availability.

1. HEATING FOR STORAGE, PUMPING AND INJECTION

Heavy fuels need to be heated during storage for several reasons:

a) The efficiency of the settling process, dropping out of water and sediments, is enhanced at higher temperatures. Maintaining a settling tank at betweeen 60°C and 70°C is therefore recommended.

b) Fuels should be held in storage at least 10°C above their pour point to prevent solidification. Wax deposits may coat heating coils forming an insulating layer and making reheat difficult.

c) To allow satisfactory pumping heat must be applied to reduce the viscosity. The minimum temperature needed may be obtained from Chart No. I.

Fuel heating for pumping and injection

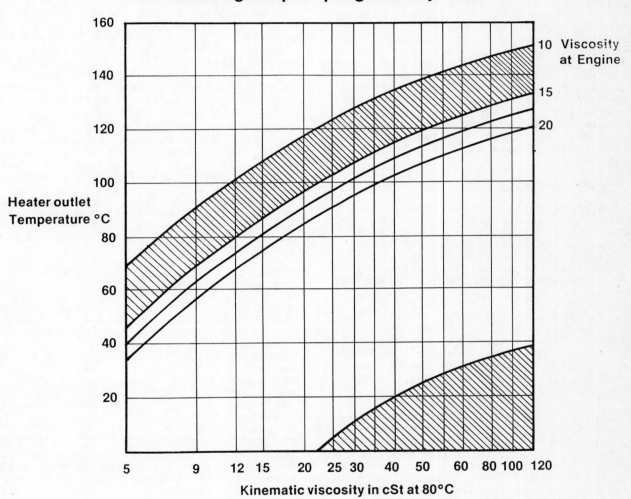

Shaded area: Pumping becomes difficult or impossible

Pumping: The fuel oil should be maintained at a temperature above that where pumping becomes difficult, eg. viscosity at 80°C = 40cSt minimum temperature for pumping is 20°C

Injection Viscosity: To achieve an injection viscosity between 10 and 15 cSt, the temperature should be maintained within the upper shaded area, eg. 50 cSt fuel at 80°C should be heated to 127°C for 12cSt at injection.

Chart 1

As an example fuel with a viscosity of 45 cSt at 80°C (Approx 180 cSt at 50°C) would need to be raised to at least 22°C to facilitate pumping.

A 380 cSt fuel (79 Cst at 80°C) would need to be at least 35°C for transfer.

Purification

As residual fuel oils may contain impurities such as water and sediments, it is essential that effective centrifuging is conducted. The setting of centrifuges is critical and the makers handbook should be referred to. However, it is necessary to heat these fuels to around 98°C for optimum centrifuge performance. Conventional centrifuges are designed to treat fuels with densities up to a maximum of 0.991 kg/C at 15°C. Veritas have found that although Shipowners have ordered fuels with this density limit, many deliveries are found to have densities approaching or exceeding 1.000 kg/l. With such high densities, the conventional centrifuge acts merely as a pump, the quality of the fuel being unchanged from inlet to outlet.

Injection Viscosity

The diesel engine injection viscosity should be between 10 and 15 cSt for correct ignition and atomization. Heating to achieve the required viscosity may be achieved manually if the operator is aware of the actual fuel viscosity or more accurately by automatic viscosity control.

With reference to Chart I, it can be seen that the 180 cSt fuel (45 cSt at 80°C) would need to be heated to approximately 128°C for injection, whereas a 380 cSt fuel (79 cSt at 80°C) would need to be at approximately 135°C to achieve a similar viscosity at injection.

It is clear that in addition to the above additional heating costs that heavy fuel oil treatment plant will need more maintenance than that operated on a distillate fuel. In addition to this the sludge and water removed during treatment must be disposed of. This in itself can create additional costs unless an incinerator is used as part of the fuel heating system. It is essential that water and sludges are completely removed from the fuel circuit and not merely transferred from one tank to another as they will eventually find their way to the engine.

2. POTENTIAL INCREASE IN FUEL RELATED ENGINE PROBLEMS

Engine builders will produce a 'heavy fuel' specification which would have been developed as a result of trials conducted on engines. This should be used as the basis for fuel selection. However, consideration must be given to the type and effectiveness of the fuel treatment plant. The end user may purchase fuels which have contaminent levels above the engine requirements if he is confident that these contaminents can be reduced to engine acceptable limits in the treatment plant.

In the following, the writer has attempted to address the important factors of heavy fuel purchasing, storing treatment and burning and identify the quality parameters which affect each process.

Unfortunately, fuel suppliers rarely provide a detailed analysis report for the fuels they wish to sell. They will usually provide density, viscosity, sulphur and water levels but metals, ash and sediments are not often reported.

Ordering by viscosity alone provides very little information with respect to overall fuel quality. Our experience with marine fuels has shown that high level of ash and sediment may be found in 180 cSt fuel and 380 cSt material.

Lower viscosity fuels are more expensive as they are more heavily blended with distillate, however, this can sometimes cause instability leading to heavy sludging during the treatment process.

The purchaser of heavy fuels should not be deterred by the lack of quality data provided by the supplier and should always attempt to purchase against a specification.

Table No. 5 provides an example of an ordering specification.

Table No. 5

FUEL PURCHASING SPECIFICATION	
Viscosity @ 50°C	380 cst – Max 400
Density @ 15°C Max	0.991
Water MAX	1.0%
Ash MAX	0.15%
SHF MAX	0.15%
Vanadium MAX	600 ppm
Sulphur MAX	5.0%

Although the purchaser may have ordered to a specification he should not assume that he will receive a fuel which meets that requirement. By analysing data over many years VPS have found that approximately one in eight of our fuel deliveries fail to meet acceptable standards on at least one parameter.

The only way to be sure of fuel quality received is to arrange for independent laboratory testing. This information will not only show whether the ordered quality has been received, but will also provide data which will allow the engineer to heat and treat the fuel correctly. If the laboratory finds that the fuel is of such poor quality that engine or plant damage could result, the power station would be able to take corrective action and avoid such damage.

There is a risk that if fuels of unknown quality are mixed in storage that separation or layering may take place and heavy sludge may precipitate to the tank bottom.

If mixing is unavoidable, due to storage limitations, a test should be conducted on the two fuels to ensure that they are compatible before mixing is conducted.

Often Fuel Suppliers will deliver two grades of fuel, e.g. a distillate and a residual fuel and blend them during delivery. Unless this blending process is correctly carried out, a homogenous fuel will not be created. Delivering one road car of diesel and 9 cars of heavy fuel into one tank and trusting that they will mix correctly should not be tolerated. Layering of the fuel in the storage tank is likely under these conditions and correct treatment of the fuel would be impossible.

Removal of Sediment and Water

Correct heating during storage will promote separation of water from the fuel. In addition, depending upon the storage period, a proportion of the sediments will settle out.

Centrifuging of low quality fuels however, is considered an essential part of treatment. This process may consist of two elements namely separation and clarification.

The term clarification refers to that process whereby solids are separated from a liquid. If the centrifuge is set up to operate in this way, it is termed a clarifier. In addition, a similar machine can be operated to remove water and solids - separator.

In both these procedures it is essential that the machine internals are set correctly and that the fuel to be treated is delivered at the correct temperature. To achieve this, the operator should be aware of the fuel density. The centrifuge manufacturers will provide instructions for correct use of their equipment and these need to be carefully followed if efficient cleaning is to be achieved.

Heavy sludging of separators can occur if the fuel is unstable. This is usually as a result of indiscriminate blending of fuels.

Water

The water content of the oil entering the separator will depend upon the degree of settling achieved in the storage tanks. Agitation of the fuel between the settling tank and separator may, however, cause emulsification. Water separation under these conditions may become impossible and every effort should be made to provide streamline flow from the settling tank to the centrifuge. In order to check the performance of the centrifuge, analysis of fuel for water before and after the separator should be conducted from time to time.

Sediment

An indication of the sediment content of the fuel will assist the engineer in determining the quantity of sludge and deposits which will be extracted during the separation process. The sediment level obtained by analysis gives an indication of the oil insoluble residues which are made up from sand, rust, scale etc. Efficient centrifuging will remove the majority of these contaminants, but some particles of catalytic fines, may not be removed. The SHF or Sediment by Hot Filtration result also provides an indication of the fuel stability. Levels above 0.15 would indicate that the asphaltines in the fuel are precipitating to form a sludge.

It is important to ensure that centrifuges are cleaned on a regular basis or their efficiency will deteriorate.

Abrasive Fine Particle Contaminants

Even with efficient fuel oil separation and clarification, a certain amount of fine abrasive particles will be contained in the fuel oil.

As fuel suppliers give no indication of the amounts or type of such contaminants in their delivery notes and unless the operator arranges for independent fuel analysis, he will be totally unwaware of potential problems.

In addition to sand, rust and general dirt, the fuel may contain aluminium silicate(s) particles carried over from the catalytic cracking process. These fines are extremely hard amd may be present in the fuel in sizes between 1 and 150 microns. It is suggested that fuel clarification, if conducted at a low flow rate, may remove a high percentage of these particles (particularly those in the 20-30 micron range. As the fines are porous and have a low relative density, however, centrifugal separation cannot be guaranteed.

The fuel filters must, therefore, be designed to remove those fine particles which have not been extracted in the clarifier. The filters also act as a safety measure if the separation plant becomes defective and allows carry over.

Filters which remove particles down to 5 microns may be recommended by the engine designers and there are many types and sizes to choose from. The care and maintenance of the fuel oil filters is important and the suppliers' instructions should be adhered to if effective filtration is to be achieved.

It should be remembered that particles of aluminium and silicon (catalytic fines) may cause severe engine damage. There have been cases of extreme wear in the fuel injection systems, cylinder liners and piston rings.

The above notes refer to the importance of efficient cleaning of the fuel to remove solids and water, however some contaminents cannot be removed from the fuel by mechanical means but their presence may lead to severe engine damages. In some cases fuel additives may prove helpful but generally the fuel user should attempt to limit the risk of such damages by careful fuel ordering, fuel quality analysis and correct engine thermal conditions.

Carbon

Although carbon deposits will always be generated, even in a well run and maintained engine, poor atomisation and subsequent incomplete combustion will create late burning, high exhaust temperatures and general overheating of valves, pistons, rings and liners. The increased amount of carbon will deposit on the above components, resulting in higher wear rates.

Carbon deposits also tend to combine with any ash which may deposit on the valves and valve seats. These deposits will be "hammered" by the valve opening and closing action causing erosion of the metal. The sealing faces of the valves are then destroyed and passages are created across the valves which allow the hot combustion gases to pass. These passages are then made deeper and wider by the escaping high velocity gases.

Vanadium/Sodium

The most corrosive of the ashes formed are vanadium pentoxide and sodium sulphate. As the ratio of vanadium to sodium will affect the temperature at which these corrosive ashes deposit, some engine manufacturers will add to their fuel specification not only the levels of vanadium and sodium acceptable, but also the limiting ratio. With a ratio of vanadium/sodium of three, the stiction temperature may be as low as $330^{\circ}C$.

As the vanadium level cannot, economically, be reduced the removal of sodium becomes essential. Sea water contamination of the fuel should, therefore, be avoided and the separation plant operated effectively to reduce the water content of the fuel.

If sample analysis reveals high levels of ash, further tests should be conducted to identify its components.

The usual effect of vanadium and sodium ashes on a diesel engine is the burning out of exhaust valves. Once these ashes have adhered to the valve sealing surface, they tend to attract other carbon and ash deposits which in turn cause impact damage. This process being a combination of mechanical and thermal fatigue and corrosion.

Engine damages caused by sodium/vanadium ashes are not limited to exhaust valves and deposits may also form on piston crowns and turbo-charger grids, nozzle rings and blades.

Sulphur

Sulphur will be present in most fuel oils, the content varying between 1 and 6%. The sulphur content of the fuel will affect the gross heating value. For example, a fuel with an API gravity of 33 has a heating value of 19,530 Btu/lb with a sulphur content of 2.5% by weight. If the percentage sulphur is increased to 5%, however, the gross heating value is reduced to 19,270 Btu/lb. The engineer will probably be more interested in the effects of sulphur during and after the combustion process.

The production of sulphurous acid and sulphuric acid will depend on the amount of water vapour present, the amount of excess air and the temperature. Basically, these acids are formed when the gases are taken below their dew points. For sulphurous acid development this temperature ranges between $50^{\circ}C$ and $60^{\circ}C$ and for sulphuric acid between $110^{\circ}C$ and $150^{\circ}C$. These acids will cause corrosion in the lower temperature zones, hence the effect is often referred to as "cold end corrosion".

In order to combat the acidity caused by sulphur, engine lubricating oils have been developed with a high reserve of alkalinity. This reserve being indicated by the Total Base Number of the oil (TBN).

The effects on the engine components, of using a high sulphur content fuel may not only be restricted to corrosion of liners, piston rings and grooves and valve stems, but may be apparent in the gas side of the turbo-chargers. The formation of sulphate deposits in the combustion space may also lead to increased wear rates.

The combustion process is a complex matter, in which the fuel quality plays an important role. Not all the defects and problems encountered, however, may be solely attributed to fuel quality.

If the fuel burning equipment is not maintained and set correctly, poor or incomplete combustion will take place and symptoms similar to those outlined above will result. If cylinder liners, exhaust valves and injectors are not maintained at optimum temperatures, corrosion and deposit formation will develop.

The selection of a correct TBN lubricating oil and the maintenance of an optimum oil feed rate will reduce the corrosive wear of components. If the oil consumption is reduced below maker's recommended values, the alkalinity will be reduced as less new oil is being added to the engine.

If the engine is run at low loads for prolonged periods then the maker's instructions should be referred to, as increased fouling may become a problem.

Fall off in the performance of the air charging system will affect combustion and careful monitoring of this equipment is, therefore, essential.

Ignition Quality

With most distillate fuels, it is possible to establish a cetane index which indicates the ignition delay period of the fuel. As residual fuels may not be homogeneous and have complex molecular structures, the determination of this value becomes more difficult.

The cetane number of a fuel is measured during engine tests and the cetane index is calculated from the API gravity and the mid boiling point of the fuel. A high cetane index indicates a short ignition delay but it should be remembered that, although a blended heavy fuel may have a short ignition delay due to the distillate component of the fuel, this does not mean that combustion will be complete and good.

If fuel with a long ignition delay is used in slow speed engines, the efficiency will be affected since the maximum peak pressures will be reduced. The effect on medium and high speed engines may be more serious with longer ignition delays causing excessive shock loads on pistons and rings and could result in ring failure and possibly bearing and crankshaft damage.

Poor ignition quality in residual fuels can be reasonably well predicted by the Shell CCAI (Calculated Carbon Aromaticity Index).

$$CCAI = d - 81 - 141 \log \log (V \times 0.85)$$

Where d = density kg/m^3 at 15°C

V = viscosity centistokes at 50°C.

In short, this indicates that levels with high density and relatively low viscosity have a high CCAI value and hence could be expected to have a longer ignition delay.

However, it cannot be overstressed that correct engine cylinder temperatures, optimum injector performance and correct injection viscosity have a considerable effect on the ignition and combustion process.

Veritas Petroleum Services provide their customers with CLAI values on completion of analysis and generally comment when the level exceeds 860. However, the engine operator should check with the engine builders if he experiences ignition problems.

Summary

With reference to the following, the reader will be able to identify which parameters of fuel quality should be considered at each stage of fuel handling between purchasing and combustion.

STAGE	POSSIBLE PROBLEMS	ACTIONS
Fuel Ordering	Viscosity of fuel will not give any indication of levels of contaminents in fuel	Develop and use a fuel specification to suit the engine and treatment plant.
Determination of delivered quantities	Incorrect density advice could result in overpayment	Use analysis result of density to calculate weight of fuel delivered.
Fuel Delivery	Fuel may be unstable and or incompatible with fuel already held in storage. This could lead to heavy sludging during storage or treatment. Mechanical cleaning of the tank would be expensive.	Test for stability and compatability before mixing. Avoid mixing wherever possible.
	Blending of fuel may not give a homogeneous product.	Do not rely on blending in tanks.
Fuel Storage	Fuel needs to be stored at correct temperature to promote settling of water and to allow pumping. Overheating is expensive. Underheating of high pour fuels may result in wax deposition and extreme difficulties when attempting to reheat prior to transfer. Tank cleaning could then be the only solution.	Analysis of fuel sample will provide viscosity and pour point from which correct heating levels may be determined.

STAGE	POSSIBLE PROBLEMS	ACTIONS
Water removal during storage.	Water could build up in storage tanks and be pumped into the fuel system. Salt water could react with the vanadium in the fuel to cause low melting point ashes leading to exhaust valve failure.	Check water drains frequently and regularly Fuel analysis results will immediately identify any deliveries with high water content. Ensure water and sludges are correctly disposed and not circulated.
Separation	Incorrect heating of oil and wrong setting of centrifuges will result in poor separation of solids and water.	Use analysis results of density and viscosity to determine correct temperature for separation. Also refer to machinery manual for correct internal settings.
Fuel Injection	Incorrect heating for injection could result in poor atomization and combustion leading to deposit formation and damage to valves, rings turbo chargers etc.	Use viscosity analysis results to determine correct injection temperature. Use automatic viscometers rather than temperature control especially for machines which operate on variable loads.
Ignition	Some residual fuels may have poor ignition quality which could lead to engine knocking and in serious cases severe engine damage. Especially on medium and high speed engines.	Observe CCAI value and maintain engine charge air temperature correctly. Ensure injection equipment is in good order. Do not run engine on low loads.
Combustion	Residual fuel blends contain various levels of contaminents which may cause:- Severe engine wear eg. liners, piston rings, fuel pumps and injectors. In addition high levels of sulphur may lead to cold corrosion. High levels of vanadium and sodium could lead to high temperature corrosion. Carbon build up could foul internals leading to component failure.	Use fuel quality analysis to determine levels of contaminents. If fuel cannot be adequately treated and is outside ordered specification it should not be used. Rejection of a low quality fuel may seem an expensive operation but if fuel analysis shows severe engine damage could be caused this may be the only commercial decision. Some problems can be resolved by using chemicals but it is essential that correct mixing and dosage be maintained.

Monitoring treatment plant performance

The storage tanks, filters and separators all perform a vital role in the treatment of fuels. If the performance of any of these falls off, the fuel will not be adequately treated and engine damages may be caused.

Fuel samples from key positions around the fuel treatment plant should be taken at regular intervals and submitted for analysis. Corrective action can then be taken if it is revealed that any component is not working at optimum conditions.

Some of the problems identified from routine samples of ships fuel treatment systems are listed below:-

1) Water build up in storage tanks.

2) Sediment build up in storage tanks. Including high levels of aluminium and silicon.

3) Steam heating coils in storage tanks leaking - increasing water content during storage.

4) Incorrect centrifuge operation:- centrifuge merely acting as a pump and not treating the fuel. This is due to incorrect settings or the operator not being aware of the fuel density.

5) Filters not operating correctly. Wrong elements fitted and incorrect cleaning schedules.

The Shipping Industry has turned to fuel testing by specialists as a matter of routine, saving operational costs and predicting problems before they arrive. Perhaps it is timely for the diesel power stations around the world to consider the same approach.

Conclusion

The use of lower grade fuels for diesel engines can be cost effective providing the user developes a sound fuel management system. The operating staff must be fully aware of the problems if machinery damage is to be minimised.

Due to the fact that refineries all round the world are slowly upgrading their plants to include catalytic and thermal cracking it is not safe to assume that because fuel quality in one area has been good for some years that it will remain so in the future.

Acknowledgements

The writer would like to thank the staff of Veritas Petroleum Services for their assistance in producing this paper. Material has been collected from the three VPS laboratories (Oslo, Teaneck USA and Singapore). In addition data and technical notes have been extracted from papers presented by VPS technical staff in London, New York, Hamburg, Rotterdam and Singapore.

Case Histories

To emphasise the importance of monitoring fuel quality deliveries, I have included three case histories where poor quality fuels were delivered to ocean going vessels.

CASE 1

A shipowner participating in the Veritas programme sent to our Teaneck laboratory a fuel sample that was taken whilst bunkering at a US west coast port. The analysis data we obtained was reported to the shipowner and he complained to the fuel supplier because the fuel had an ash content of 0.24%, an aluminium content of 55 mg/kg, a silicon content of 108 mg/kg, and was unfilterable in the sediment hot filtration test. Some additional information about the fuel is given below.

The fuel supplier sent his retained sample to Laboratory E and on being advised that the ash, aluminium and silicon contents were low and within acceptable limits, the fuel supplier rejected the shipowners complaint. Laboratory E obtained levels of ash, aluminium and silicon, see column 2 in the Table, much lower than we had obtained on the sample taken by the ships personnel.

The shipowner was not satisfied and when the vessel reached Singapore he decided to send the fuel sample given to the ship by the supplier to Laboratory F for testing. The ash and aluminium contents obtained by Laboratory F, see column 3, were very different to those obtained on other samples tested by Laboratory E and ourselves. It is recognised that the sample tested by us was different as it was taken by the ship's staff, but the two samples analysed by Laboratories E and F should have been the same provided the supplier had taken one large sample and split it into two, one to retain himself and the other to give to the ship.

The shipowner then decided to tell Laboratory F to send what remained of the sample they had tested to the Veritas laboratory in Singapore. Our results are given in column 4. The similarity in the analysis results determined in our laboratories between the samples taken by the ship's staff and the supplier shows that both samples were very similar and the main reason for the shipowners complaint against the supplier of high ash, high aluminium and an unfilterable fuel was fully justified.

The supplier agreed to have the fuel offlifted at his expense.

This incident illustrates one of the benefits to the purchaser of marine fuels, and also the shipowner for his chartered ships, in having all fuel deliveries analysed by a worldwide organistion dedicated to maintaining a high standard of quality controls.

CASE 2

A motorship bunkered IF 380 at a northern European port and the fuel sample taken by the ship's staff during the delivery was sent to us for analysis. Some of the data obtained is listed.

Density at 15°C g/ml	0.990
Viscosity Kinemtic at 50°C cSt	229
Aluminium mg/kg	35
Silicon mg/kg	32

It would appear the supplier took a very responsible attitude in delivering a fuel with a viscosity much below the maximum permitted for IF 380 in order to meet a density of 0.991 at 15°C which is considered to be the upper limit for good centrifuging using conventional equipment. The aluminium content was a little higher than that mentioned in the BS MA 100 1982 publication and the shipowner reported this to the fuel supplier.

The fuel supplier replied saying that they had checked their retained sample and obtained an aluminium content of 31 mg/kg. However the supplier went on to say that they were always concerned to avoid incurring a bad name for the quality of their fuel. They considered the excessive amount of aluminium in a recently delivered product to be serious. Historically aluminium had been well within specifications and checked regularly although not on every batch of fuel. Because of this incident, they had decided to test every batch of fuel destined for motorships for aluminium before releasing it for use. They expressed their appreciation that the problem had been brought to their attention.

Such a worthwhile reaction and constructive attitude by a fuel supplier is to be commended and demonstrates quite clearly that all suppliers do not necessarily react in the same way.

CASE 3

A motorship lifted fuel in a northern European port and a fuel sample taken during the delivery was sent for analysis. Some of the results are given below.

Density at 15°C g/ml	0.974
Viscosity Kinematic at 50°C cSt	185
Water %	0.8
Conradson carbon %	13.9
Ash %	0.29
Vanadium mg/kg	73
Aluminium mg/kg	107
Iron mg/kg	252
Calcium mg/kg	275
Sediment H F %	Not filterable

The fuel purchaser complained to the fuel supplier because of the high ash content, a high aluminium content and the abnormal amounts of other metals such as iron and calcium present in the fuel. The fuel was also unstable and would cause problems during centrifuging.

The fuel supplier agreed that the fuel should be offlifted at his expense.

The vessel was on route to South America and had sufficient fuel from previous bunkers to reach there. Additional bunkers were lifted in South America but it was not possible at the port of call to remove the substandard fuel. The fuel was offlifted when the vessel was at a U.S. West Coast port.

It does not require much imagination to think of the problems that this ship would have experienced had no fuel sample been sent for prompt analysis thus initiating all the necessary precautions that needed to be taken.

Samples of IF 380 tested in four laboratories

Sample taken by	Ship	Supplier		
		Retained by supplier	Given to ship	
Testing Laboratory	Veritas USA	Lab E USA	Lab F	Veritas Singapore
Density at 15°C g/ml	0.973	–	0.973	0.974
Conradson carbon %	9.4	–	12.8	9.0
Ash %	0.24	0.06	0.03	0.26
Vanadium mg/kg	59	–	64	55
Aluminium mg/kg	55	5	24	59
Silicon mg/kg	108	11	–	114
Sediment H F %	not filterable	–	–	not filterable

Generators for diesel engine and gas turbine applications

P F NELSON, BSc, CEng, MIEE
Chief Project Engineer—Systems Engineering, NEI Peebles Limited

INTRODUCTION

The paper discusses generators for diesel engine and gas turbine generating sets in the range from 1MW to 15MW. In this range generators are generally designed for the application and to meet the users particular requirements.

Considerations appertaining to generators for either application are examined and additional comments specific to diesel or gas turbine sets made where necessary. Construction is described and a brief section on generator electrical protection is also included.

RATING

Output/Speed/Number of Sets

The number of sets and the rating depend on a whole range of factors including power requirements, fuel type and prime mover outputs. Usually the generator manufacturer is simply advised of the output and number of sets required.

generator speed will be determined by the prime mover and system frequency;

gas turbine generators in the range under discussion usually run at 4 pole speed i.e. 1500 rev/min (50Hz) or 1800 rev/min (60Hz);

broadly speaking 'high speed' diesel generators run at 1500 or 1000 rev/min (50Hz), 1800 or 1200 rev/min (60Hz);

'medium speed' between 750 and 500 rev/min (50Hz) or between 900 and 514 rev/min (60Hz);

'low speed' below these speeds.

The relative merits of the different diesel speeds is outwith the scope of this paper. The following generalisations should however be noted

a) the smaller output sets tend to run at higher speeds and the larger output sets at lower speeds.

b) for the same output the higher speed generator will cost less than the lower speed.

The maintenance requirements for the diesel or gas turbine are greater than for the generator and therefore flexibility considerations become significant when deciding on the number of sets required. The points following should be considered in specifying the generator rating.

Duty

It is the responsibility of the purchaser to declare the duty as accurately as possible and the manufacturer to then assign a rating. Generators are usually specified as duty type S1 (continuous running duty) and assigned a 'maximum continuous' rating (MCR) in accordance with part 101 of BS4999. Duty type S2 'short-time duty' might be advised for some applications, resulting in a 'short time' rating S2 60 min, with the time indicating the operating period.

It is important to specify any requirements to start motors which are large relative to the size of the generator as discussed further under reactances.

Cooling Medium Inlet Temperatures

As generator outputs are limited by temperature rises it is essential that the cooling medium temperature is advised. It is also important that the method of stator temperature rise measurement, i.e. by resistance or by embedded temperature detector, is either specified or agreed at the time of order. Rotor temperature rise is always by resistance for practical reasons.

Insulation Class and Temperature Rise

Modern insulation systems are generally Class F and are therefore rated for a total temperature of 155°C although improved materials mean that elements of the system may carry higher ratings thus increasing their reliability and longevity.

In order to maximise insulation life, the practice has been to limit temperature rise to the lower Class B limit i.e. 80°C rise by resistance, 85°C by embedded temperature detector (ETD) over air inlet temperature of 40°C for stator windings and 90°C by resistance for strip on edge rotor windings. While this practice continues, the improvement in insulation materials makes it possible to specify class F rises i.e. 100°C by resistance, 105°C by ETD over an air inlet temperature of 40°C for stator windings and 110°C by resistance for strip on edge rotor windings. This is particularly evident in circumstances where a higher continuous rating is only required for part of the year or under particular conditions. The implications of ambient temperature relative to gas turbine performance and hence generator rating are discussed later.

On generators with water cooled heat exchangers, temperature rise can alternatively be (and normally is) measured over cooling water inlet temperature providing this does not exceed 25°C. The permitted Class B and Class F rises are then increased by 10°C.

Increased temperature rises are permitted in section 16 of BS4999 part 101 by agreement between the manufacturer and purchaser. They can be increased by the amount which the air inlet temperature is lower than 40°C or the cooling water is below 25°C but with a maximum increase in temperature rise of 30°C.

Gas Turbine Generator Rating

The rated output of a gas turbine is normally the output at an ambient of 15°C. Its output increases as the ambient temperature decreases and vice versa. The maximum output is limited by the gearbox rating which might correspond to the gas turbine output at approximately -10°C.

The curve for generator output against inlet ambient temperature for Class B rise corresponds reasonably to the turbine output curve. BS4999 part 101 however has a break point at 10°C which prevents the generator manufacturer from declaring any increase in output for inlet air temperatures below 10°C.

Depending on the application, expected minimum temperatures etc, it may be that the generator rating should be chosen as the maximum gas turbine output (based on minimum temperature or gearbox limit) with a Class B rise over an inlet air temperature of 10°C. Works tests can then verify this performance with validity in respect of BS4999 and there is the assurance that Class B rises will be maintained for all gas turbine outputs.

On a generator with an air to water heat exchanger, the output is generally considered constant given a maximum cooling water temperature. The rating has therefore to be chosen to correspond to a particular point on the gas turbine curve, say the ISO rating point of 15°C, and Class F temperature rises allowed for the higher gas turbine outputs at lower ambient temperatures.

Gas turbine generator rating is therefore a matter for discussion between the gas turbine and generator manufacturers and the end user to ensure that the right balance between cost and performance is achieved.

The generator designer also has to consider reactance and stability at the higher outputs based on the low ambient temperatures.

CONSTRUCTION

Stator

The core comprises high quality, low electrical loss sheet steel laminations, insulated on one side to restrict eddy current losses. Following punching of the slots, the laminations are deburred and built up on one of the core end-plates, with a number of ventilation air passages included within the length of the core. At intervals during building, the laminations are pressed down and finally, when the correct length of core has been built, the second core end-plate is put in place and pressure applied to clamp the core. Pressure is maintained on the teeth between the slots by means of tooth-support fingers which are spot-welded to double thickness laminations. A similar arrangement is used to form the radial ducts built into the core to serve as air passages. Core pressure is maintained using long back of core bolts or bars welded between the core end plates (in the latter case the bars are also welded to the core packets) or by welding the 'top' core end plate into the stator frame where single piece laminations have been fitted into a machined barrel type frame.

The stator winding is usually of the two layer lap type comprising pre-formed diamond shaped coils inserted into open slots. The coils are secured in the slots by wedges driven into grooves located at the top of the stator slots and the winding overhang is braced by glass fibre support rings and inter-coil blocking. The coil insulation is mica based and the insulation system is either resin rich or vacuum pressure impregnated (VPI), each of which have advantages. The surface of the slot portion of coils in generators operating over 4.2kV have a semi-conducting coating or tape which earths the surface of the coil to the core thus avoiding corona discharge and subsequent failure.

Rotors

Salient pole rotors are manufactured in two types. Firstly, for high-speed machines with 4 or 6 poles, the rotor is made from a single steel forging. The pole bodies are machined to provide a seating for the field coils which are held in place by means of solid, high-tensile steel pole tips, bolted on to the pole bodies. Secondly, machines with 8 or more poles are manufactured with laminated steel poles which carry the field coils and are either bolted on to the shaft assembly or, for high peripheral speeds, may be held in place with an integral T-section or a single dovetail. A cage winding is built into the pole face of each laminated pole to give the damping effect necessary for satisfactory operation in parallel with other synchronous machines, especially with shaft systems in which there is an inherent cyclic variation in torque, as with diesel engine driven generators.

The field coils for the solid pole type of rotor are of the fabricated, strip-on-edge construction, with rectangular corners at which brazed dovetail joints are made. Epoxy resin bonded nomex is used as insulation between the turns of the coil. Each coil is heated under a pressure which is greater than that due to the centrifugal force on the coil when rotating at the maximum over-speed. After curing, the coil dimensions are such that the pole tip will clamp the coil on the pole body when it is bolted down. The size, number and arrangement of pole tip bolts is chosen after design analysis of the stresses which will be established in the pole tip. Additional support for the field coils is provided by clamps located between the poles to prevent any circumferential movement of the conductors due to centrifugal force.

For laminated pole rotors, the field coils are either of the strip-on-edge type or are wound directly on to the poles, using a relatively small, pre-insulated rectangular conductor. Such coils are of the multi-layer type, with interleaved glass tape and epoxy varnish being used to provide support and binding for the field coil, which is fully oven-cured. Again, when necessary, clamps are provided between the poles to prevent movement of the conductors in the coils.

Bearings

Sleeve bearings are generally used for generators in the range under discussion although rolling element bearings are quite common on the smaller sizes.

Gas turbine generators are frequently of the two bearing type although on the smaller sizes single bearing (at the non-drive end) design with the turbine gearbox overhung on the generator stator frame has gained popularity due to its compact arrangement.

Diesel generators are in most cases single bearing designs with the driven end solidly coupled to the diesel flywheel.

Generator sleeve bearings are generally of the oil ring type and are usually flood lubricated from the diesel gas turbine lubrication oil system.

To prevent shaft currents causing pitting of the journals the non-driven end bearing is insulated from the bedplate/stator frame. On two bearing machines the driven end bearing is also insulated but earthed with a copper strap which can be removed to allow testing of the bearing insulation.

VOLTAGE

Preferred Values

The preferred values are those typically occurring such as 415V, 3.3kV, 6.6kV, 11kV at 50Hz, and 440V, 4.16kV, 13.8kV at 60Hz although strictly speaking BS4999 refers only to machines with voltages derived from the nominal voltages given in IEC 38: Standard Voltages.

System Considerations

The actual voltage chosen will in practice depend on a number of factors including the voltage of the system or equipment to which the generator is to be connected, system and switchgear fault levels and cost.

Manufacturing and Cost Implications

In simple terms the lower output machines are most economically manufactured at lower voltages and the higher output machines at the high voltages. There are no hard and fast rules but the following will illustrate:

A 1MW 11kV machine has small cross-section stator winding copper conductors which are

difficult to insulate to the required voltage. If a high voltage generator is preferred, it would be manufactured more economically at 3.3kV and a unit transformer utilised to change to 11kV.

A 2MW, 415V generator will require considerable stator winding copper and will probably be more economically manufactured at 3.3kV.

A 10MW, 3.3kV generator will similarly be more economically manufactured at 6.6kV or 11kV.

REACTANCES

Direct and Quadrature Axes

Reactance figures given for electrical machines relate to a theory put forward by Park in the 1920's. This theory analysed machine reactances along the centre line of the rotor poles (where the air gap is smallest) known as the direct axis and along the centre line of the gap between the rotor poles (where the air gap is largest) known as the quadrature axis.

From the users point of view it is usually the direct axis reactances that are considered.

Direct Axis Synchronous Reactance, Xd

Xd is the ratio of the excitation current required to give full load stator current with the machine on short-circuit to the excitation current required to give full voltage on the machine on open circuit, neglecting saturation.

If this ratio was unity the machine would be said to have 1 per unit direct axis synchronous reactance. Another way of looking at this is to take the voltage produced on open circuit and divide it by the current produced on short circuit with the same excitation current as was used for the open circuit voltage test. Volts divided by current is obviously impedance and since resistance in the stator is really very low, impedance can be considered as reactance. If V and I are expressed as fractions of normal V and I which are valued at unity, a per unit value will result. If real V and I are used the value of Xd will be in ohms.

The saturated value of the direct axis synchronous reactance is denoted Xd sat. It is always less than the value of Xd due to the bending of the magnetisation curve. The short circuit ratio (SCR) is the reciprocal of Xd sat.

Direct Axis Transient Reactance, X'd

When a sudden change of load takes place on a generator the effect in voltage dip is very much less than the value of Xd would suggest. This is because the flux in the salient pole cannot change its value quickly due to the long time constant of the field system. This reactance is the direct axis transient reactance X'd.

Direct Axis Subtransient Reactance, X"d

If one looks very closely at the voltage dip occurring on a change of load, right at the very beginning of the period following the change of load the drop in voltage is even smaller than the value of X'd would indicate. This reactance is the direct axis subtransient reactance X"d and is due to the damping effect of either solid pole tips or cage damper windings in the pole tips.

System Significance and Generator Capability

In a.c. generators of modern design where no special characteristics have been requested, the direct axis synchronous reactance Xd will be quite high, typically of the order of 2 per unit for high speed generators, and 1.35 per unit for medium speed generators. This means that hand control of the excitation is only suitable for emergency operation and for this reason control of voltage and kVAr sharing is achieved by a fast acting solid state regulating system.

In addition however, it also means that the ability of the unit to operate under line charging conditions is rather limited. This is shown on the steady state capability diagram in figure 1. Where small units are installed in remote areas, the ability to provide charging current for cables and overhead lines in the area under abnormal conditions may be important.

The values of X'd and X"d are important for two reasons. Firstly X'd is used for determination of maximum voltage drop on application of load and it is common to have a maximum value specified. The value of X"d can be important in relation to the maximum fault current which the generator is allowed to contribute to the system and it is common to specify a minimum value.

When both these aspects are considered, the result is that X'd is specified with no upward tolerance and X"d with no downward tolerance. Since X'd and X"d are closely tied together magnetically, the designer can have great difficulty in achieving a satisfactory design. If only one value is critical the designer will move the design point to get a safety margin.

Figure 1 shows a power chart or steady state capability diagram for a typical synchronous generator. The small circle on the left is constructed by determining the extremities from 1/Xd and 1/Xq. The diagram is actually constructed for Xd = 1.7 and Xq = 1.0 (a reasonable ratio). From this it can be seen why a requirement to run at leading power factors can necessitate a low value of Xd and hence an increase in frame size.

Relative Costs

Returning to the definition of Xd, if the full load current of a given machine is reduced to 50% of its previous value, the machine hasn't changed, the ohmic value of Xd has not changed but the per unit value has halved. In other words, the allocated rating of a machine relative to its actual physical dimensions affects the reactance value. The bigger the machine for a given rating and speed the lower will be its reactance. Of course, making the machine larger will reduce its temperature rise and in general increase its efficiency.

1   STATOR HEATING LIMIT
2   ROTOR HEATING LIMIT
3   TURBINE OUTPUT LIMIT
4   ZERO EXCITATION
5   MINIMUM EXCITATION
6   THEORETICAL STABILITY LIMIT
7   PRACTICAL STABILITY LIMIT

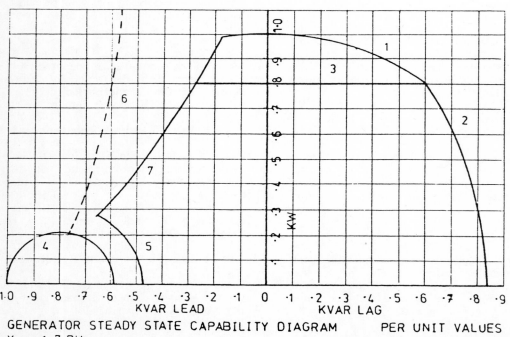

GENERATOR STEADY STATE CAPABILITY DIAGRAM   PER UNIT VALUES
X_d = 1.7 P.U.

Fig 1

It is possible to vary X'd and X"d for a given value of Xd, but this is a more difficult phenomenon to explain, as are the effects on efficiency. It relates to changing flux and saturation levels within the machine and is too complex to be discussed here.

ENCLOSURE AND COOLING METHOD

Classification

Enclosure classifications are closely related to cooling methods and hence to cooling classifications since the achievement of higher degrees of protection in terms of enclosure classifications necessitates certain cooling methods and precludes others.

The IP System of Enclosure Classification is fairly widely known, where the first digit represents the degree of protection against contact with live or moving parts and the ingress of solid foreign bodies; and the second digit represents the degree of protection against harmful ingress of water. For generators, the system is detailed in Part 20 (to be superseded by part 105 in due course) of BS4999. The IP ratings of various enclosure types are mentioned in the paragraphs that follow.

The classification of methods of cooling detailed in Part 106 of BS4999 is perhaps less well known to those involved with generators for gas turbine and diesel applications than the terms used in the following paragraph headings.

Screen Protected Drip-proof (SPDP)

This is the simplest form of enclosure cooling with a shaft driven fan or fans drawing air into the machine passing it over the windings and exhausting it back into the surrounding atmosphere.

The enclosure classification is typically IP22 (protection against contact by finger and ingress of particles greater than 12mm diameter, protection against water drops falling any angle up to 15° from vertical and the cooling classification ICA01.

The user has to ensure that a) there is adequate ventilation to dissipate the generator losses b) the inlet air is sufficiently 'clean' to avoid blocking cooling circuit airways (or be prepared to clean them out regularly which increases maintenance costs).

Filter Ventilated (FV)

A filter ventilated generator is similar to an SPDP machine except that filters are fitted on the air inlet(s) (and sometimes also on the outlets) to prevent ingress of dust, fibres etc. The enclosure classification remains IP22 if only inlet filters are used but is raised to IP43 if outlet filters and louvres on the inlet and outlet are also fitted. The cooling classification remains ICA01.

The possible problem of heat dissipation remains but the difficulty of dust etc in the airways is overcome. Filters however have to be changed from time to time. Differential pressure switches are sometimes fitted to sense filter blockage. If airborne contamination is at a very high level, the frequency of filter replacement would make filter ventilation an unsuitable choice.

Closed Air Circuit Water Cooled (CACW)

With a closed air circuit water cooled generator the primary coolant, namely air, is circulated through the machine by shaft mounted fan(s) and passed through an air-to-water heat exchanger generally mounted on top of the generator to cool it before circulating through the generator again.

The enclosure classification is typically raised to IPW54 (protected against harmful quantities of dust, protected against splashing water) and the cooling method classification is ICW37A81.

Such a generator is therefore suitable for working in 'dirty' conditions but obviously a suitable source of cooling water will be required.

Emergency doors to open-ventilate the generator in the event of cooling water failure are often specified.

Closed Air Circuit Air Cooled (CACA)

This is similar to the CACW generator except that the air-to-water heat exchanger is replaced with an air-to-air heat exchanger. The degree of protection is again classified as IPW55 and the cooling classification is ICA01A. On generators, electrically driven fans are generally used to circulate the external air since the shaft mounted exciter makes the use of a shaft driven external fan more difficult.

This arrangement is again very suitable for dirty environments, but if located indoors, requires dissipation of the generator losses from the building.

Cost Implications

The SPDP machine will clearly be the least expensive with only a small increase for the addition of filters. There is an appreciable increase in generator size due to the addition of an air-to-water heat exchanger on the CACW generator but the generator frame size will probably remain the same.

Retrofitting of air-to-water heat exchangers has been carried out on several installations where the conditions have proved unsatisfactory for an SPDP generator without reduction in generator rating. The CACA generator requires a larger frame size for the same output and this combined with the cost of the air-to-air heat exchanger makes it the most expensive option.

The user therefore has to balance the various factors listed above in reaching an economic decision. If noise is also a consideration then the CACW generator is the quietest option although acoustic treatment can be undertaken on the other options.

GENERATOR MOUNTED MONITORING AND AUXILIARY EQUIPMENT

Stator Embedded Temperature Detectors

The use of embedded temperature detectors, either thermocouples or resistance temperature detectors (RTD's), has become almost universal. Typically two per phase are normally specified and two or three spares are usually fitted, as replacement of a failed detector is not feasible.

Monitoring is often by means of a single instrument with alarm and trip set points and a selector switch. The operator records the stator temperatures every half hour and leaves the switch selected to monitor the highest temperature in between times. Periodic study of the trends in the recorded stator temperatures along with the ambient and/or cooling water temperatures can give usual indications that the air passages or coolers require cleaning while the instrument set points protect against continued overload, cooling medium problems or similar.

With the increasing trend in unmanned installations and in the fitting of temperature detectors in other parts of the machine, multipoint temperature monitors with individual alarm and trip set points are being increasingly used. Recording (possibly less frequently) and study of trends in the temperatures remains a worthwhile exercise.

Cooling Circuit Thermometers and Probes

In addition to stator temperature detectors, thermometers (usually with alarm and trip set points) or temperature probes (RTD or thermocouple) are common on larger generators in the inlet and outlet air circuits and sometimes where applicable in the cooling water circuits. Where temperature probes are utilised, a multipoint temperature monitor as described above would be required.

Bearing Thermometers and Temperature Probes

On generators with journal bearings, again either thermometers with alarm and trip set points or temperature probes are used. The thermometers or probes usually measure the bush temperature close to the white metal.

On smaller generators with ball and roller bearings temperature monitoring equipment is usually not fitted but, if required, is of the thermocouple or RTD type, since space considerations preclude the use of mercury-in-steel thermometers.

Vibration Monitoring

Partly as a result of the increasing prevalance of remotely controlled generators and partly as a result of greater availability of economically priced detectors, the fitting of vibration monitoring has become common prctice on gas turbine generators but not on diesels.

The range of equipment available is considerable, the cost increasing with the degree of sophistication.

The simplest units bolt to the top of the bearing and have an alarm or trip contact with an inhibit circuit for start up.

The first progression is to fit an accelerometer (or two at right angles) to the bearing with a remote instrument giving continuous indication, and monitoring against alarm and trip set points.

The most sophisticated units have a pair of proximity probes mounted radially at right angles to each other on the bearings with the probes directly monitoring shaft movement.

Anti-Condensation Heaters

On machines which may be inactive for periods when temperature and humidity conditions would lead to moisture condensing on the interior surfaces of the machine, low-voltage heating units are fitted in the stator frame to maintain internal air temperature at a level which will inhibit condensation. The heaters are normally automatically switched on by circuit breaker auxiliary contacts when the generator is out of service.

EXCITATION SYSTEM

Basic Principles

The salient pole rotor has a d.c. field winding. The excitation system provides and controls the d.c. power to the field winding and hence controls the generator voltage before synchronising and the reactive power output/power factor after synchronising.

Traditionally d.c. was supplied to the field via sliprings from a d.c. exciter. On many of these generators the d.c. exciter is being replaced with a fully static thyristor excitation system deriving its power from an auxiliary transformer connected to the generator terminals.

Brushless Excitation

Modern generators for diesel and gas turbine sets usually employ a brushless excitation system. On a brushless a.c generator, the d.c. exciter is replaced by a revolving armature a.c. machine, the output of which is rectified by a rotating diode assembly. From the rectifier, a d.c. supply is fed direct to the revolving field system of the main a.c. generator by leads passing along the shaft. The whole of the excitation circuit is therefore solidly interconnected and results in the advantageous elimination of commutators, sliprings and their associated brushgear. The excitation power for the exciter can be derived from the main generator terminals via transformers or from a permanent magnet generator (PMG) direct driven from the generator shaft. The latter method is considered preferable as it enables the excitation system power supply to be divorced from main supply system disturbances. This is important when operating under fault conditions since a short circuit on the generator line terminals could remove excitation from the machine at a time when maintenance of fault current is required to give satisfactory operation of the protection relays. The latter consideration means that machines whose excitation is derived from the machine terminals must have special current transformers fitted if short circuit current maintenance is to be provided.

The basic circuit of the brushless exciter system with permanent magnet generator is shown in figure 2. The permanent magnet generator provides a power supply for the main exciter, which is controlled by a thyristor automatic voltage regulator (AVR) or alternatively, under emergency conditions, by a hand adjusted variable transformer and rectifier unit or by a manually adjusted electronic control unit. The generator field is therefore controlled by varying the a.c. exciter field. The silicon diodes used in the rotating rectifier are conservatively rated and are selected to withstand the stresses imposed by transient fault conditions such as a sudden short circuit at the machine terminals.

In view of the high reliability of modern semi conductor devices and their satisfactory performance in machines already built, it is considered unnecessary to incorporate rotating fuses for protection against diode failure. Such fuses are fitted however, if specifically required by the client. On large machines (approximately 6MVA and above) a rotating resistor is permanently connected across the output of the diode bridge to limit to a safe value any induced voltages which could occur during faulty operation such as synchronising out-of-phase.

Generator Capability Diagram

Reference has already been made to the generator characteristics and to the steady state capability diagram.

The steady state operating point on the capability diagram is determined by the governing system in the vertical power axis and the excitation system in the horizontal reactive power axis. It can then be appreciated that too high a value of excitation will result in excessive rotor heating while too low a value of excitation will result in unstable operation of the generator.

Electronic Automatic Voltage Regulators

Modern electronic automatic voltage regulators (AVR's) typically comprise half controlled bridges with the output determined by the error signal from a circuit which compares the generator voltage via a sensing voltage transformer (VT) and the AVR set voltage.

AVR voltage setting is typically by adjusting a potentiometer which can be motorised for remote control or automatic synchronising. Some recent designs have an internal voltage setting circuit with adjustable rate of voltage trimming making them suitable for local or remote control without additional components. A compounding circuit fed from a current transformer (CT) in the generator line is usually provided to enable stable VAr sharing when operating in parallel with other sets or a power system. With suitable generator design the AVR response can be virtually instantaneous.

Automatic Power Factor/kVAr Control and Other Features

Depending on the degree of supervision the excitation control system can be enhanced by the addition of various control and protective features. These are either in the form of

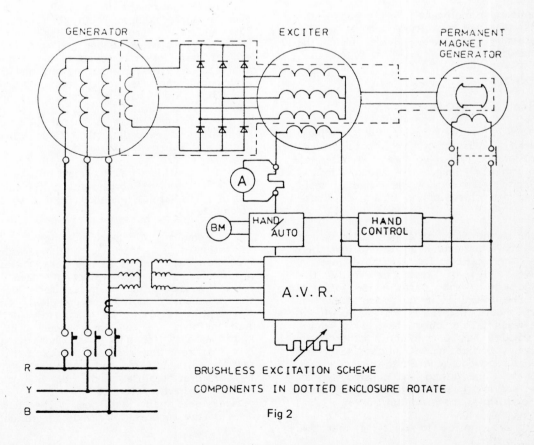

BRUSHLESS EXCITATION SCHEME
COMPONENTS IN DOTTED ENCLOSURE ROTATE

Fig 2

additional PCB cards or modules and include:

overexcitation limit to prevent excessive rotor heating and minimum kVAr limit to prevent unstable operation on a generator running in parallel with a power system where changes in system voltage will tend to cause changes of generated kVAr which may otherwise take operation outside safe limits;

diode failure detection which can distinguish between open and short circuit diodes and be arranged to alarm in the event of an open circuit diode and to trip the set in the case of short circuit diode when excessive exciter heating would result;

AVR fault detection arranged to trip the generator to hand control when the output current and voltage are inconsistent with the generator operating condition;

V/Hz control unit to prevent overfluxing of the generator during start-up or shutdown if it is desired to leave the excitation connected;

constant power factor or constant kVAr control for operating in parallel with the grid or other large power system.

When operating in parallel with the grid, constant kVAr operation is often chosen as it minimises import of kVAr from the power supply with the resulting tariff advantages regardless of generator kW load. Some constant kVAr controllers include a kVAr shed feature which can be initiated when load is reduced below a certain level. Reversion to voltage control when the grid tie is lost and during run-up/shutdown is usually achieved by means of circuit breaker auxiliary contacts.

It is therefore important to specify the requirements for the excitation control system and if necessary, to seek advice from the generator manufacturer.

WORKS TESTING

Classification

These can be categorised under two headings: tests to verify satisfactory manufacture, e.g. insulation resistance, high voltage and tests to verify performance, e.g. no load losses, temperature rise, efficiency. The range of tests to be carried are classified as Basic, Duplicate and Routine.

If a machine is the first of a particular design (or the first for a particular power station) then basic tests are called for - these are a comprehensive series of tests to verify the design, manufacture and performance of the generator. The meaning of the term 'basic' in this context should therefore not be confused with its use when talking about, say, a car where the 'basic' model has a minimal, rather than comprehensive, specification. Duplicate tests are specified for subsequent generators to verify that they are of the same design and construction as the machine previously subjected to 'basic' tests and also to confirm sound manufacture.

Routine tests are limited to verifying that the generator is in sound working order and able to withstand the high voltage test. They are normally considered insufficient for the range of generators under consideration.

The requirements for basic and routine tests are defined in part 143 of BS4999.

Basic

Basic tests comprise measurement of winding resistance, no load losses, temperature rises, high voltage, vibration, short circuit saturation and losses or zero power factor test.

Duplicate

Duplicate tests comprise measurement of winding resistance, no load losses, high voltage and short circuit saturation only.

Additional

Additional tests are only carried out if specified by the purchaser, either directly, or by requiring the manufacturer to guarantee certain generator characteristics such as noise, reactances. Additional tests which can be specified include noise, telephone harmonic factor and sudden short circuit.

Methods

The methods employed to carry out many of the tests such as resistance measurement, high voltage and vibration are fairly self-evident. The method of determining efficiency for generators in the range under consideration is usually by summation of losses. This is detailed in section 11 of part 102 of BS4999.

The losses measured in a series of tests, and over an agreed range of outputs (typically 100%, 75% and 50%), are iron, windage and friction, stator copper, rotor copper and excitation. The sum of these losses is added to the output of the generator to give the input power, and hence the efficiency can be calculated. Synchronous reactance (X_d) is derived from the short circuit characteristic obtained by driving the generator at rated speed short circuited at the stator terminals and recording the stator current with decreasing values of excitation.

The transient and subtransient reactances, X'_d and X''_d, and the corresponding time constants, T'_d and T''_d, are determined from a sudden short circuit test.

The element of testing where there are limitations is that of temperature rise measurement. It is not generally possible or practicable to run generators at rated load and power factor in the manufacturer's works but the methods adopted nevertheless allow the temperature rise to be accurately determined. Two methods are commonly used. The first is known as a two part kVA run when the generator is run at zero power factor overexcited firstly at rated voltage, reduced current until the temperature stabilises and then immediately at rated current, reduced volts until the temperature again stabilises. The temperature rises of the generator are thus determined.

The second method, which is usually only adopted on larger generators where test facility limitations prevent a two part kVA run, involves the summation of the temperature rises resulting from unexcited, open circuit and short circuit heat runs, to determine the total temperature rises of the generator.

SINGLE/PARALLEL OPERATION

Principles

It is perhaps worth stating the basic factors in terms of single/parallel operation although most will be familiar with them.

Single Running

- the generator controls the speed/frequency, the power output (MW) is determined by the connected load.

- the AVR controls the voltage, the reactive power output (MVAr) and power factor (cos Θ) are determined by the connected load.

Parallel Operation - before synchronising

- the governor controls the speed/frequency

- the AVR controls the voltage

                    - after synchronising to large/stiff system

- the governor controls the output (MW), the system controls the frequency.

- the AVR controls the reactive power output (MAVr) and hence power factor (Cos Θ), the system controls the voltage.

                    - after synchronising to small/weak system

- the governor controls the output MW and also affects the frequency.

- the AVR controls the reactive power output but also affects the voltage.

The settings of the various AVR's of the generators on the system have therefore to be such that there is reasonable sharing of the reactive load and at the same time the voltage is maintained at the required level. Too high a total reactive power output from the sets will cause the system voltage to rise and too low will cause the voltage to fall.

The same applies in terms of the governors with respect to total power output and system frequency.

Control

The above comments make it clear that satisfactory control of frequency and power is dependant on the governor system which is outside the scope of this paper.

Similarly, satisfactory control of voltage and reactive power/power factor is dependant on the excitation control system. The preceding section has discussed this topic in some detail. It is

therefore sufficient to say that as a minimum, the AVR will require a compounding CT and a droop characteristic for parallel operation.

Adjustment of the AVR setting on loading the generator can then achieve satisfactory VAR loading/sharing. On automatic schemes or where there is minimal operator supervision, the use of a constant kVAr or power factor regulator should be considered.

Comment has been made earlier on the requirement for laminated poles with damping windings on diesel generators to give satisfactory parallel operation.

PROTECTION RELAYS

Essential

When considering protection relay requirements, what is regarded as essential is a somewhat subjective matter and is influenced by the size of the generator and the application.

Differential or Circulating Current protection has become virtually universal on generators above 1 to 2MW and is generally applied above 1MW. This is a change from the situation of 25 years ago when the recommendation was for its application on generators over 5MW. The high speed action of the differential relay can minimise the damage to the core in the event of an internal fault in the generator. On larger generators the more sophisticated but inevitably more expensive biased differential relay is often used.

Reverse Power protection is always fitted, the required sensitivity depending on the application - the power required for the generator to 'motor' a diesel engine will be appreciably greater than for a gas turbine of the same rating. A timer to prevent spurious tripping following synchronising is required and is often an integral part of the reverse power relay. It is the prime mover manufacturer's responsibility to define the minimum 'motoring' power. It is worth mentioning that measurement rather than protection accuracy CT's are required particularly for the more sensitive reverse power relays.

Overcurrent protection is usually of the inverse definite minimum time (IDMT) type. On generators, the voltage controlled or the voltage restraint type is frequently specified.

The type of stator earth fault relay employed depends on the method of generator earthing. If it is solidly or low resistance earthed then an IDMT overcurrent relay is used in conjunction with a CT mounted after the generator star point. If it is high impedance earthing by means of a distribution transformer connected to the generator star point, then an overvoltage relay is used, either IDMT or definite time, connected across the transformer secondary loading resistor.

Where generators are connected to the grid on which there is auto-reclosing equipment, loss of grid protection is specified to prevent out of synchronism reconnection by the auto reclose.

Additional Relays

The following relays can perhaps be put in this category.

Field failure relay - the AVR may already include an AVR failure detector which will trip the excitation to hand if the AVR fails.

Negative phase sequence overcurrent - this relay detects levels of negative phase sequence current higher than the generator has been designed to withstand due to unbalanced loads or faults on the system.

Overvoltage protection is sometimes fitted to protect against sustained overvoltage due to a failure of the excitation control equipment or incorrect operation in hand control.

Electronic or Electromechanical

Until about 5 years ago electronic protection relays were viewed with considerable suspicion by many engineers. They have however become much more widely acceptable offering in some cases additional features or greater versatility for the same price. The wider use of modular systems combined with more compact electronic designs has also increased their acceptability. The range of available electronic protection relays continues to increase but the situation still arises where all but one relay in a generator protection scheme is of modular construction and the one electromechanical relay takes up almost the same space.

Electromechanical relays still have the advantages of familiarity for many and are also favoured where the application is remote from specialist electronic test and repair facilities.

SITE COMMISSIONING

Minimum Requirement

As a minimum site commissioning of the generator should include

1. Check for satisfactory alignment with prime mover.

2. Insulation resistance test on the stator, rotor, main exciter and excitation PMG. If possible bearing insulation should also be checked.

3. When carrying out 2, a polarisation index test on the stator winding, the polarisation index being the ratio of the insulation resistance value at 10 minutes to the value at 1 minute. It should normally exceed 1.6.

4. Verification of control equipment operation as far as possible without the set running.

5. Check that all terminations correct, generator and surrounding area clear of all debris and then that all coverwork fitted.

6. Initial run with generator unexcited to verify bearings satisfactory.

7. Initial excitation control setting up - firstly in hand and then in AVR control (in accordance with AVR manufacturer's instructions).

8. Phase rotation and synchronising checks.

9. Following synchronising and/or connection to load, further setting up of the excitation control equipment, in particular the limit units if fitted.

10. Full load run to verify that temperature rises are satisfactory and to enable setting of temperature alarms and trips.

Additional Tests

Additional tests can include:

1. High voltage test at 80% of factory test value - usually not considered necessary, particularly on generators delivered to site fully assembled.

2. Short circuit run - sometimes required to dry out generator insulation if the resistance values are low.

3. Vibration measurements - often these are only carried out if qualitative indications suggest vibration levels are excessive.

CONCLUSION

Only through an understanding of the various aspects of generators and associated equipment discussed in this paper will diesel and gas turbine engineers be able to specify generators that meet the users requirements and operate them to best advantage.

ACKNOWLEDGEMENTS

The author thanks his colleagues for assistance in proof reading of the text and NEI Peebles Ltd for provision of photographs.

AUTHOR

The author is Chief Project Engineer in the Systems Engineering department of Peebles Electrical Machines, NEI Peebles Ltd, Edinburgh, Scotland. Following graduate training with Scottish Engineering Training Scheme, in 1974 the author joined NEI Peebles where he has worked on a wide range of power generation projects.

Fig 3   One of sixteen 500 r/min, 11kV diesel engine driven salient pole a.c. generators for 2 UK power stations (8 × 5.2MW and 8 × 6.735)

Fig 4   One of three 1.25MW, 4.16kV, 1800 r/min, gas turbine driven brushless a.c. generators for an oil production platform

Fig 5   Partially assembled 5500kW, 6.6kV, 1500 r/min a.c. generator

Fig 6   Rotor with laminated poles and fully interconnected damper winding

Civil engineering for diesel and gas-turbine power stations

R D MAYHEW, CEng, MIStructE
Kennedy and Donkin Power Systems Limited
G P WELLS, CEng, DIC, FICE
Consulting Engineer

Introduction

In the construction of any power station, 'Civil Works' can be taken, broadly, to include all those items of work which are necessary to provide a suitable environment for the long life and satisfactory operation of the plant. At the same time it is necessary to consider the needs of the operating staff, the adjacent landowners, and the environment generally.

Thus the civil engineer must not only design the structures to support and protect the plant and operating personnel, but must also address external problems such as noise barriers and landscaping. Road improvements to cater for the fuelling traffic and access for plant and construction equipment must also be considered.

The requirements of diesel and gas-turbine power units are often similar, but some manufacturers of gas-turbine sets have developed accoustic shields for their machines which, in benign climates, can be enhanced to act as weather shields also thus reducing, or removing the need in some cases for a full-scale power house (Fig.1).

A large proportion of the total fuel energy is discharged to atmosphere through the exhaust gases. It is, therefore, often economically practical to recover some of this heat, through waste heat boilers, as steam for further generation, desalination or for industrial processes. This involves the civil engineer in the design of the necessary water intakes and processing plant as well as the extensive additional foundation works. However, it is not considered that this work should form part of this paper.

Civil engineering considerations seldom govern the selection of the site since the cost of the civil works is at most about 25% of the total station costs. However, such items should be considered as part of the selection process because, cumulatively, they can become significant. The additional foundation costs resulting from poor sub-soil alone can be as much as 10% of the civil costs, or $2\frac{1}{2}$% of the total.

The requirements and opportunities offered by the selected site will, to a large degree, dictate the extent of the civil works: the need for noise attenuation, the height of the exhausts, the availability of river or sea water for cooling, the fuelling route and so on.

General

The civil engineering design of a diesel or gas-turbine power station must primarily be concerned with ensuring the long life and satisfactory functioning of the plant.

Thus sound and durable structures on well engineered foundations, using high standard materials and finishings are crucial. To achieve this it is first vital that the owner and plant supplier provide clear statements of the space requirements of the plant, and of the loads, both static and dynamic, which will be applied to the structures. In order for the civil engineer to design a satisfactory Power Station it is essential that his mechanical and electrical engineering colleagues co-operate to ensure that this information is made available at the commencement of the design period. Too often the information is late arriving or is incorrect and requires alteration late in the programme to the detriment of the design and/or the progress on site.

Further discussion will be required with the owner to discover the extent of facilities required, and with the Local Authorities to establish other design parameters concerning environmental and siting considerations.

To achieve durable structures careful thought must be given to the selection of materials. Concrete aggregates must be tested fully to avoid the risk of alkali-aggregate reaction and alkali-silica reaction. The availability of all materials must be verified to ensure continuity and consistency of supplies. Strict supervision of the workmanship and continual surveillance of the materials brought onto the site is vital if the works are to be durable; this applies especially to the concrete materials, production, placing and curing, but is also important for all other areas of the work.

Soils and ground water must be tested for aggressive chemical content, and precautions taken to protect the structure against their effects. In such conditions the cement used for all underground concrete may have to be sulphate resisting or the faces of all concrete in contact with soils protected by enclosure in polythene sheeting or painting with bitumen. In particularly severe conditions it may be necessary to use epoxy-coated reinforcing bars or a combination of all three protective measures.

Broadly, the civil engineering design can be divided into four main areas:

i.   The Power House

ii.   The Engine/Alternator foundation blocks

iii. Outdoor foundations and other on-site facilities

iv.   Off-site considerations.

The site selection process must include desk studies of available geotechnical and seismic data of the area. As soon as possible a full and thorough geological investigation programme should be put in hand; this should include drilling, coring and sampling, and testing, in-situ and in the laboratory, to establish the strength, elastic properties and dynamic response of the sub-soils, local irregularities and the extent of any problems caused by high or aggressive ground water.

The data thus obtained must become the basis of the design of foundations and structures. Loads are relatively heavy, and power stations are frequently relegated to the less attractive sites, thus piling or some form of ground improvement, for example through dynamic compaction or vibro-compaction, is frequently required. The dynamic nature of the loads applied, not only by the prime plant but also by some ancillary items of plant, and the danger of propagation of ground-borne vibrations from the main plant must be taken into account in the foundation design.

Where water cooling is to be adopted, or waste heat is to be recovered, investigations in similar detail must be made into the quality and reliability of the water supply.

Power House

The power house must provide a controlled environment helping to ensure the long life of the plant and satisfactory working conditions for the staff. It is likely that a new station will have to be designed with a view to future extensions, and the materials selected and structural connections provided at the first stage must facilitate the later works.

Apart from architectural considerations, factors affecting the selection of construction materials include environmental conditions and availability, but typically the power house will comprise steel portal frames with 'lean-to' annexes at the sides to house electrical and mechanical equipment and facilities. Walls and roof are usually of insulated profiled metal sheeting although the lower 2m of walls is often of rendered blockwork to afford some protection against mechanical damage; where the climate is appropriate fibre-cement sheeting is an acceptable and cheaper alternative. Floors must be hardened to provide a dust-free surface, and concrete surfaces liable to oil contamination must be sealed. In urban situations the need to control noise is likely to dictate the use of concrete block walls and reinforced concrete roofing.

The insulated profiled metal sheeting may be of steel or aluminium. In aggressive environments it is essential that steel sheeting is heavily galvanised and provided with high build special polyurethane, PVF2, or similar long life corrosion resisting system. The wall system can be either built-up, with outer layer profiled sheet, loose insulation material on battens and sheet steel inner tray, or a rigid sandwich comprising similar inner and outer sheets but fully bonded together with a rigid polyisocyanurate foam. This latter has the additional advantage that intersticial condensation problems are eliminated.

Aluminium sheets may be used instead of steel sheets. Aluminium has a natural resistance to corrosion but is softer and liable to mechanical damage and distortion resulting from inaccurately driven fixings; it is also subject to electrolytic corrosion if allowed to come into contact with steel in damp conditions (e.g. condensation). It should therefore be isolated from the steel frame using PVC tape, a paint film is not considered sufficiently reliable for this purpose.

Noise levels close to the units within the power house are likely to be in the order of 110 dB; these are unlikely to reduce with distance without careful selection of wall materials to absorb some of the energy. A reduction of about 10 dB can be attained by the use of accoustic linings to walls and roof; ear defenders of high quality are essential for maintenance operatives. Quietened cabins close to the units housing local controls can provide oases of calm for the operating personnel, but it is now felt desirable to remove these controls from the power house.

The structure must be capable of resisting all static and dynamic loads imposed by the plant and equipment, as well as those imposed naturally by wind, earthquake etc, without adversely affecting the operation of the plant. Because of its size and the conditions inside the building when the station is in operation, maintenance of the structure is difficult. Hence particular attention must be given to the selection of all finishes to ensure a long life to first maintenance. Structural steelwork must be provided with a first-class corrosion protection system; as a minimum the steel should be blast cleaned to the standard of SA2½ before coating with one of the many long-life paint systems available today; alternatively, the steel may be galvanised and painted. It is usual nowadays for the final top coat of paint on structural steelwork to be an intumescent paint to add some further measure of protection from the effect of fire.

Natural and artificial lighting, heating and cooling facilities are installed according to the requirements of the location; in adverse conditions it is frequently necessary to introduce forced ventilation at a higher than ambient pressure to reduce the risk of dust penetration. Ventilating air is drawn in at low level, through filters if necessary, and released at roof level through vented sheeting. The resulting internal over-pressure helps in combating dust problems in the station.

Fire detection and fire fighting equipment should be designed to limit the spread of any fire to a single unit, without unduly affecting the performance of adjacent units unnecessarily.

Large doors are required to facilitate plant access. Where particularly aggressive conditions are likely to occur these must be made dust resistant and possibly even combined with an isolated loading bay. Careful attention to detail is important to ensure that openings are effectively sealed if noise levels outside the station are to be controlled; this applies not only to doors and windows but also to the junctions between wall panels and in the roof sheeting. Sound attenuating ventilation louvres must be used and all openings for pipes, cables etc. must be sealed.

For all but the smallest units it is necessary to install an overhead travelling crane of suitable capacity to lift the largest single element of the plant. This crane must have a slow moving or creep facility to enable heavy loads to be placed accurately without risk of damage; in turn, this places constraints on the permissible deflection of the structural frame.

The engine/alternator sets are housed under a single span portal frame. Sufficient lay-down space is provided between sets to enable maintenance work to be undertaken without interruption to the safe running of adjacent units. This space is usually similar to that required by the sets themselves. The lay-down areas are designed for an equivalent distributed load in the order of 15 kN/sq.m. or more as required to enable major refitting work to be undertaken. At the same time trenches and ducts must be formed in the slab to carry pipework and cables.

In order to reduce the tendency to propagate ground-borne vibrations, the sides of the foundations should be isolated from the surrounding soil. Since the cost of excavating the soil between the bases is likely to be less than the cost of forming separating walls, this has led to the development of layouts for diesel stations which include full basements. The resulting space enables the anti-vibration mattress or springs to be kept dry and maintained, and eases drainage problems. Small plant and equipment, heavy fuel oil heaters and pumps, lubricating oil tanks, pipe runs etc. are conveniently housed in the basement, thus permitting the engine room floor areas to be uncluttered and clear of trenches. Fire fighting equipment must be specified to suit the conditions and the plant installed, and must minimise the risk of fire spread.

The disadvantages of the basement layout are the additional cost, and the fact that the laydown areas between the units at ground level must be supported from the basement floor. (Fig.2)

Ideally the control room is placed in a position where all units can be seen, often above the electrical annexe, but access is usually arranged to be from outside the power house. Particular attention is paid to the reduction of noise penetration into this room. The electrical annexe will contain other necessary staff facilities, the battery room, LVAC room and so on.

Because the large voltages generated can cause dangerously large differences in potential between structure and ground under fault conditions, all stanchions must be connected to the site earthing grid. This must be installed at shallow depth throughout the site as far as the boundary fence which should also be connected.

Engine/Alternator Foundations

The engine foundations have the dual functions of supporting the generating set and of preventing, or minimising, the propagation of ground-borne vibrations. At all times the function is to maintain the rotating shafts in correct alignment. This imposes strict limits on flexure and differential settlements.

In addition to static forces, the foundations must be designed to resist the large vibrational forces causing oscillating flexural stresses, and the forces due to differential thermal expansion of engine and foundation. Details of the factors to be considered and guidance for the designer are to be found in BS2012, the Code of Practice for Foundations for Machinery.

The foundations must also be capable of withstanding the effects of occasional short-circuit and faulty synchronisation torque forces without detriment.

It is the responsibility of the plant supplier to provide the foundation designer with all details of the loads imposed by his plant. In addition to the static loads he must provide all necessary data relating to the dynamic characteristics of the unit when running.

Depending largely on the type of sub-soil available and the size and dynamic characteristics of the unit there are three main types of foundation in common use, (Fig.3), each of which may be divided into many sub-types:

a) Generating set bolted to top of heavy block of reinforced concrete which is supported directly on the foundation material and is in contact with soils at the sides.

b) As above but with the reinforced concrete block supported on springs, or other damping system, set on reinforced concrete foundations (piled if necessary).

c) Generating unit fixed to steel sub-frame mounted on springs, or other damping system, set on reinforced concrete foundation.

Foundations for diesel engines installed in the past were frequently designed with side slots or tunnels to provide access for fixing nuts to the concealed ends of holding-down bolts. These discontinuities inevitably caused stresses to be raised locally, and, for convenience, contractors often formed construction joints at the same level, causing complete separation of the concrete which reinforcement alone could not counteract (Fig.4).

In all cases the reinforced concrete should be designed without re-entrant angles and cast in a single continuous pour. Where holes or slots are unavoidable they should be rounded as far as possible to minimise stress raisers. In this way reinforcing bars or prestressing cables can be arranged to pass straight from face to face, or nearly so, in three directions.

The pouring of large volumes of concrete creates problems of control of internal temperatures, and of the resulting thermal stresses. These can be reduced by the use of retarding agents and cooling water circuits cast into the block. The required high strength concrete can be produced relatively easily, but transporting, placing and, especially, curing of the finished product is always more difficult. Uncontrolled stresses due to thermal gradients in immature concrete cause internal cracking with resultant loss of integrity. Resistance to this internal stressing is assisted by the introduction of reinforcement in three directions at close centres throughout the concrete in addition to that required near the surfaces to resist flexural and torsional stresses.

In designing the holding-down system for the generating set precautions must also be taken to eliminate the effects of differential or delayed expansion of engine and concrete. The underside of the engine block should be ground flat and smooth, greased to prevent bonding, and set on a resin bonded non-shrink grout. In this way the engine is able to expand readily before the concrete has warmed to working temperature. The bending in the concrete due to thermal gradients is less significant and may be further reduced if direct heat transfer from engine to concrete is limited by ensuring a minimum contact area.

Under conditions of repeated stress reversal, concrete suffers cracking due to fatigue. Such cracks can occur even if tension does not develop, but have been found after less than 1,000,000 cycles (as little as 3 days running at 450 rpm) in tension zones. Where plain round bars have been used there is a rapid and progressive loss of bond along the bar resulting in a widening of the cracks; deformed bars will delay this process; prestressing to eliminate tension in the concrete will further delay the opening of the first cracks.

The sub-soil investigation should discover the elastic characteristics and dynamic response of the ground as well as its capacity for static loads. Compaction or piling is usually necessary to avoid settlement, and more importantly differential settlements, under the vibrating loads to be supported. The effect of possible saturation by fuel oil should also be examined at this stage although the block and adjacent floor should be designed to minimise or prevent such contamination.

Outdoor Facilities

For reasons of convenience, safety and/or efficiency many items of ancillary plant are placed outside the power house.

In urban conditions it is likely that limits on the overall noise level emanating from the station will be imposed by the planning authorities. Although the greatest noise comes from the power house, the various items of plant placed outside the building combine to add significantly to the whole nuisance. This will lead to the assessment of the noise output of all items of outdoor plant and equipment at tender stage, since it is often less difficult to deal with the noise source than with the effects.

Cooling radiators for lubricating oil and, in the case of diesel engines for charge air and jacket coolant, are placed carefully to avoid recirculation of warmed air. Accoustic screens may also be required around the radiator compound. Where adequate supplies of cold water are available they can be used effectively as the coolant and result in less noise than air cooling.

The generator transformers are usually placed outside the power house to guard against the risk of fire or blast effects. They are separated from each other and other items of plant by blast walls and each is provided with independent fire fighting equipment. Each transformer is provided with a separate foundation which is arranged to form a bund of sufficient capacity to retain the cooling oil and quench fires in the event of a tank burst.

Exhausts from gas-turbine and smaller diesel engines are usually supported by the plant. In the case of larger diesel plant, however, and where waste heat recovery is proposed, the stacks are provided with separate foundations.

The fuel storage area is kept well away from the plant. Except where the consequences of loss of the entire generating capacity of the station would represent an acceptable risk, tanks are normally provided with separate bunds so that a fire in one tank will not put adjacent storage in jeopardy. Bunds must be made oil-tight to prevent the contamination of subsoils and underground aquifers, and must be of sufficient capacity to retain the contents of the tank plus a margin of approximately 10% for the materials used for the fire-fighting. Independent fire fighting equipment is installed for each tank both to fight fires and to cool the tanks in the event of fire breaking out in an adjacent bund. Oil and water remaining in the bund following a fire, burst or major spillage must be removed by tankers, but arrangements are made for the removal of surface water from the bunded areas through oil separators into the site surface water drainage system.

In addition to foundations for outdoor plant items the civil engineer is required to design the various links between areas, the roads, cable trenches and pipe racks, the foul and surface water drainage systems with oil separators.

Road widths and radii must be designed for the occasional use for access of large items of plant, catering for the future replacements as well as the initial installation. The surfaces are often concrete but must be selected to resist the effects of fuel spillage from tankers. Hard-standings and tanker off-loading areas are now usually surfaced with interlocking concrete blocks, providing an easily maintained surface which is not affected by oil spillage and can be readily lifted for installation/repair of underground services.

On site, the foul and surface water drainage systems are usually kept separate; the foul effluent being treated on site or led directly into the Public Utility sewers as available. The surface water is passed through oil inter-ceptors before discharge to soak-aways. Maintenance of the interceptors remains an on-going responsibility of the station management.

Pipe racks comprise lattice steel structures and are galvanised, rather than painted, for long and maintenance-free life.

The boundary fence is frequently required to act as a security barrier as well as marking the limits of the site; in these cases a heavy chain link mesh surmounted by strands of barbed wire are the minimum requirement, and a gatehouse, with facilities for the gate-keepers must be included.

The many other minor buildings such as the offices, workshop and stores, and pumphouses will also require the detailed attention of the civil engineer. These will vary widely in size, number and function depending on the require-ments of the owner of the plant, and on its location, but as a minimum will include a small workshop and spare parts store. These will have a similar construction to the main power

house and may include a small overhead hoist. The floors will be designed for distributed loading of 15 kN/sq.m. or such heavier loading as may be appropriate to the particular plant being installed.

No power station can ever be un-noticed by the adjoining property owners; however careful detailing of the various elements comprising a new station and the provision of earth bunds or accoustic walls can reduce the noise and visual nuisance to acceptable levels.

Off-Site Considerations

The civil engineer must also address problems of access, both temporary and permanent.

During construction many heavy loads must be moved from the manufacturer's plant, or the docks, to the site; consideration must be given to the available alternatives. It is not unknown for the contractor to construct a temporary jetty out to sea rather than improve road access to his site where the necessary road works would be more costly.

Road improvements which are only desirable for the construction stage may, however, become essential for the satisfactory operation of the station, not only for the delivery of fuel, but operating staff also add to the traffic burden.

The method of transferring fuel to the station, by road, rail or sea must be shown to be adequate, or must be enhanced; the construction of an oil pipe-line or of a single-point mooring for coastal tankers may have to be considered if the available road requires excessive improvement work to make it adequate for the anticipated additional loads, or if the use of tankers would represent an unacceptable environmental disruption.

In order to enable larger tankers to use them safely, roads may have to be resurfaced, or have corners re-aligned and bridges strengthened; the economic and environmental balance between more journeys with smaller tankers against fewer journeys with larger tankers must be weighed.

Conclusions

This paper has not attempted to do more than try to point out some of the major civil and structural aspects to be considered in the design of diesel and gas-turbine power stations.

It is not, and could not be, exhaustive in its coverage. Individual situations will inevitably create different problems requiring individual solutions.

It is always essential, however, that close co-operation is maintained between the civil engineer and his colleagues in the other disci-plines. Failure to do so is likely to result in cluttered conditions and difficulties of operation.

The design of any station depends entirely on the requirements of the generating system of which it will form part. Those requirements remain paramount at all times but MUST be settled early and clearly defined.

Similarly, for the civil engineer to be able to design a satisfactory station, he MUST be in possession of all pertinent data relating to the plant from the beginning, and the suppliers of the plant must be aware of the consequences to the programme of late alterations.

The design of the station as a whole is not restricted to the power house, but must include all necessary facilities to ensure the reliable and safe generation of power.

The Authors

R. D. Mayhew is a Senior Project Civil Engineer with Kennedy & Donkin Power Systems Ltd.

G. P. Wells is a Consulting Engineer in practice in Haslemere, Surrey.

The Authors wish to thank the Directors and members of staff of The Kennedy & Donkin Group for their help in the preparation of this paper.

Fig 1   (Top) Hamba 3 MW diesel power station — United Arab Emirates
(Bottom) Two 42 MW Technologies Twinpac gas turbine alternator
sets at Dubai 'D' power station, Jebel Ali, Dubai

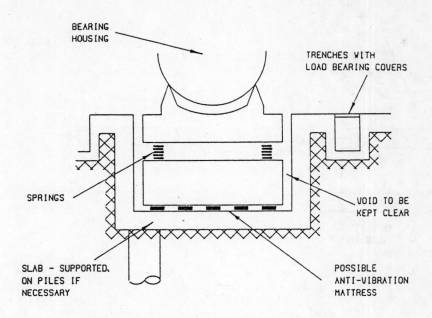

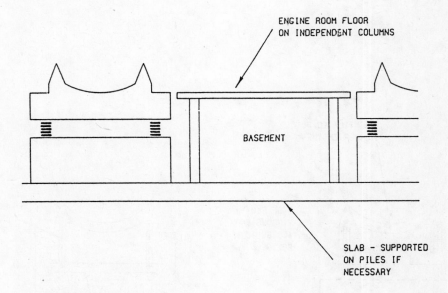

Fig 2   Alternative configurations for basement layouts

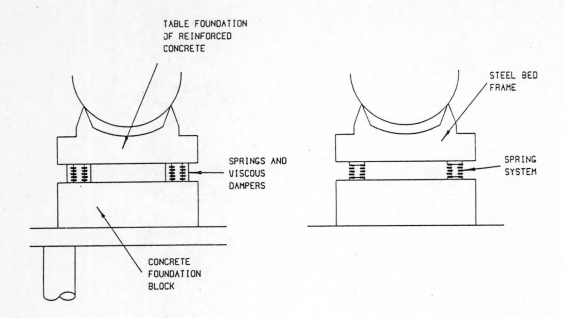

Fig 3   Typical foundation details

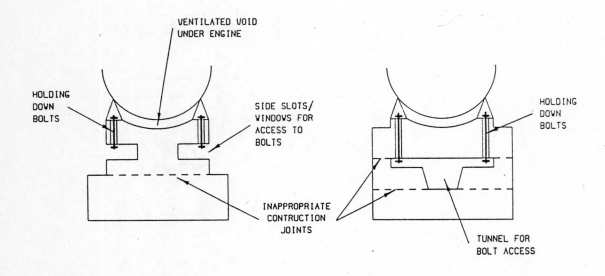

Fig 4   Older type foundations

Co-generation—CHP in industrial and commercial applications

F NASH, CEng, FIMechE, FInstE
Group Director, McLellan and Partners Limited

SYNOPSIS

The application of combined heat and power in industrial situations, 'Cogeneration', has been practised for over 100 years. It was adversely affected by the first OPEC oil price crisis of 1973 and many thought it might disappear as a result of the above combined with cheap electricity from giant nuclear and coal power stations. However, they underestimated the innovative adaptiveness of users, equipment manufacturers and system designers. Therefore 1973 also saw the start of a dynamic period of development of cogeneration systems and their application around the world. The undoubted logic of using energy as efficiently as possible received Governmental approval in 1978 via PURPA in the USA and 1983 with the Energy Act in the UK. But the greatest boost to cogeneration was the slump in primary energy prices in 1986 which makes the private generation of electricity economically attractive where a cogenerative situation exists.

Cogeneration systems can vary in size from the largest industrial power stations generating hundreds of megawatts of electricity right down to installations of a few hundred kilowatts generating capability.

Energy costs are cut because the heat produced when generating electricity is utilised rather than wasted. A variety of fuels can be used and systems work alongside existing boiler plant and local electricity supplies.

The advantages of cogeneration are available to many different process industries, typical examples are pharmaceuticals and speciality chemicals, paper, food and drink, together with large commercial buildings, computer centres, hotels and similar load centres.

The choice of plant design and configuration is largely dependent upon questions of scale and requirements for heat and power.

This paper examines the type of cogeneration systems now available, their main operational characteristics and other technical and commercial factors which must be taken into consideration in selecting a system and assessing whether or not it will be economically viable.

Introduction

Cogeneration is one of those descriptive American words written into their legislature under PURPA in the late 1970s and now has become common usage worldwide. It fundamentally covers the production of power (electricity) at high efficiency - lower limit 42.6%. The most common way of achieving such overall efficiencies is of course Combined Heat and Power, where in a fully exploited industrial installation overall conversion efficiency will average over 70%.

Most USA schemes are industrially or commercially based and perhaps in its common generic usage cogeneration should be restricted to these areas, leaving the more marginal and differently driven district heating applications to be categorised as CHP/DH.

Cogeneration is a new name for an old practice. In 1868 the construction of a newly opened sugar beet factory was reported in the technical press of the time and whereas details of the process equipment was extensively covered the reciprocating steam engine providing power and exhausting steam to the process attracted little comment as being normal practice. With the growth of the process industries, increased factory size and energy requirements, reciprocating steam engines were gradually replaced by steam turbines driven by steam produced in water tube boilers at higher pressures and temperatures.

By the early 1950s when there really was an energy crisis in the UK, industry was required to use energy more efficiently and coal-fired boilers, generally operating at pressures around 400 lb/in^2, and back-pressure steam turbines were the norm in many companies.

The availability of abundant supplies of cheap oil relieved the crisis and in general allowed energy to be considered one of the less important commodities associated with industrial production.

From 1973 with an increase in real energy costs resulting from OPEC action the efficient use of energy once more began to receive attention in all the industrial countries. This often resulted in tax incentives, grants and other legislation to encourage cogeneration.

In the UK, 1983 saw the Energy Act followed by Department of Energy part-funding of extended surveys and of installations judged to be sufficiently innovative and reproducible as to justify classification as Demonstration Projects.

These factors have however been overshadowed by the greatly increased differential between primary fuel and electricity costs caused by the world glut of oil, resulting from the OPEC-inspired general recession and user switch to other fuels, recognition of which finally became unavoidable in 1985. In consequence, interest in the local generation of electricity with high efficiency obtained by taking advantage of concurrent heat demands (cogeneration) has increased dramatically in the UK, as elsewhere, and is showing all the signs of bubbling into a mass of installations.

Factors Affecting the Selection of Systems

In the 1950s system selection was easy. It was, in the main, a coal-fired boiler and back-pressure steam turbine or nothing. Today there is a wide range of equipment available and the correct equipment and system must be selected and matched to the specific conditions and operation to produce the most economically viable plant.

Commercial viability is normally the major consideration in the selection of a system and indeed whether or not an actual installation results.

There are many interesting techno-economic factors which will determine the success or otherwise of a cogeneration system. They include:-

(a) Heat and power demand of a site (normally expressed as a ratio) and the variation in these. Whilst it is possible to alleviate the worst effects of H/P ratio variations by exporting electricity, the economic returns will be highest with the self use of all the power produced, so realising the full purchase avoidance cost

(b) The type of fuel and hence the cost of fuel the cogeneration system requires

(c) Fuel flexibility which allows costs to be negotiable

(d) The efficiency with which the cogeneration system can cope with (a) above

(e) The maintenance and operational requirements and costs of the system

(f) The specific capital cost of the system.

System Types

Cogeneration systems fall into five fundamental categories as indicated in Figure 1.

Figure 1(a) shows the classic industrial system, still the most widely used today, but which is more and more being restricted to the large process industries. It has the advantage of being able to use any fuel but unfortunately the prime cost of boilers is almost always inversely proportional to the quality (and hence cost) of the fuel burnt, ie low cost fuel = expensive boiler plant. Furthermore the system's design will be optimised not only against a fixed heat to power ratio, usually between 5 : 1 for large systems and 25+ : 1 for very small systems but also against given demands, eg 10 MW electric and 100 MW thermal outputs, and the system loses both efficiency and value of output on turndown. Any decrease in the thermal demand, say to 60 MWt in the example above will reduce the power output, by a greater than corresponding proportion, to say 5.2 MWe.

Turbines can be designed with a 'bypass' provision to feed inlet pressure steam into the second or third stage of blading which enables the turbine to absorb peaks of thermal demand and optimise performance at a lower (down to say 85% MCR) output. However, this allows alteration of one aspect of the system performance characteristic against 'KNOWN' variations at design, rather than providing true flexibility.

Figure 1(b) shows the standard method of providing flexibility to the fired boiler, steam turbine system by equipping the turbine with a condensing exhaust end. Hence the heat to power ratio achievable is variable between all the steam to the turbine being extracted (less back end cooling flow), which will typically give a H/P ratio of 8 : 1, or all steam going through to the condenser, H/P = 0. Any combination of power and thermal output is possible within the operational limitations of the turbine. Unfortunately the conversion efficiency to useful output is normally very low for steam passing to the condenser say 25%, ie worse than that achieved by a normal utility power station, and the resultant economics are such, that today these installations are only seen under special circumstances, eg a turbine driven compressor where the driving power to the compressor must be available regardless of the extraction steam to process (thermal) demand at any particular instant or often in the steel industry and oil industries where the fuel is waste gas.

Figure 1(c) indicates what is currently regarded as the system with most potential, ie an alternator driven by a gas turbine with exhaust gas waste heat recovery boiler, with or without supplementary firing.

The gas turbine is very acceptable to industry Figure 2, based on its aviation background of high power to size/low vibration levels/known acoustic treatment/high reliability/developed control and monitoring systems to minimise operator demands and, possibly most important, high availability from a quick unit exchange or major part replacement policy, operated by the manufacturers. Experience with first generation gas turbines, efficiencies typically up to 23%, has indicated that given premium fuel (natural gas) and uncontaminated air, which is not always as good in industrial situations as it is in the depths of Russia, Alaska or at 30 000 ft, maintenance costs are low.

Whilst it is almost impossible to obtain actual maintenance figures on a common basis, since even the scope of activity defined as maintenance can vary from site to site, without starting to consider different operational and accounting practices to name but three of many factors involved, experience with GTs to date indicate a figure of 0.15 p/kWhe may be considered reasonable.

Whether this will hold true for the more sophisticated second generation gas turbines (capable of up to 35% efficiency but operating at higher combustion pressures and temperatures) on offer today, only a few years in general use will show.

Under design (MCR) conditions gas turbine (GT)/waste heat (WH) boiler systems will typically operate with a heat to power ratio of 1.5 : 1 to 2.5 : 1 dependent on the prime mover installed, ie having an efficiency to power conversion of around 30% to 23% respectively.

The efficiency of gas turbines reduces quite quickly on turndown and it is normally uneconomic to operate them at much below MCR conditions in cogeneration schemes. There is considerable free oxygen in the turbine exhaust gases and supplementary firing (boost firing) is possible, theoretically to achieve H/P ratios up to 17 : 1. However, physical size and cost of ducts combined with the GTs sensitivity to increased exhaust back pressure and type of WH boiler required, usually in practice limits supplementary fired systems to a 4 : 1 H/P ratio. As with all good general rules exceptions are easily found for example where a GT is retrofitted to function as the force-draught fan supplying preheated combustion air to a boiler, furnace or dryer.

With supplementary firing the thermal output can be fully varied between the recoverable waste heat and the upper limit by simply changing the amount of boost fuel input. H/P ratios below the WHR quantity can also be achieved by bypassing exhaust gas around the boiler but this of course has a detrimental effect on system overall efficiency and the installation's economics.

Figure 1(d) indicates the same basic type of system and facilities as 1(c) above but utilises a reciprocating diesel type engine as the prime mover. This in fact changes the characteristics of the system significantly. Compared with gas turbines, engine systems have higher power generation efficiency which is retained on turndown and good fuel flexibility but present more problems as regards acoustic treatment, vibration and system complication.

Large reciprocating engines currently do not have the same acceptability to industry, as gas turbines and although pockets of preference for engines are met from time to time, generally gas turbines are preferred on the basis (perhaps from ignorance) - 'we can start them up and forget about them'. This is certainly not true with reciprocating engines, they require regular inspection and attention, whilst maintenance involves in situ work rather than total exchange. However, given that routine actions are not neglected, it is

possible that the through-life maintenance costs of larger dual fuel engines may be comparable with those of gas turbines and those of engines using distillate and residual oils only marginally higher.

Systems using automotive type spark ignition engines (Figure 3) are used successfully in swimming pools and other public buildings, their economic viability largely dependent on relatively low capital costs. Maintenance requirements are high, costing upwards of 0.7 p/kWhe and they have a limited application in industry and larger commercial installations.

It is interesting to note that perhaps only the Navies of the world have extensive comparable experience with both diesel engines and gas turbines and the latest trend is to use the latter for 'dash' only and 'cruise' on the diesels. Gas turbines, although tried, have made no headway at all into the highly cost competitive world of the Merchant Marine but this could be due more to the diesel engine's ability to operate on a variety of fuels at much higher to-power only conversion efficiencies, typically 36% to 45%, as to reliability, availability and maintenance factors in the cost comparison. These same factors are of course important in cogeneration applications, especially fuel flexibility and today base load type engines are available to operate on gaseous fuels from low calorific process to natural gas and liquids from premium diesel to the worst residual heavy oils available.

In the past engine systems have operated with waste heat recovery only where an overall H/P ratio of around 0.8 : 1 will normally be easily achieved but at two levels, ie 0.5 : 1 as steam (high quality) and 0.3 : 1 as 80°C hot water (low quality). It is not always easy to find a use for the latter. Variations in thermal demand above the 0.8 : 1 ratio level required operation in parallel of a standard fired boiler. Spark ignition engines in micro systems generally produce H/P ratio of 2 to 2.5 : 1 often with all thermal output as 65°C water.

The development of boost firing to utilise the free oxygen in a diesel or dual fuel engine exhaust extends the capability of systems incorporating medium and slow speed engines, Figure 4, to H/P ratios of 4.5 : 1 with total flexibility, and is very important to engine cogeneration systems prospects. Much will rest on the experience obtained from the UK D of E demonstration project at Cyanamid (GB) Ltd's site, Project Profile 299, where a 3.5 MWe dual fuel engine driven alternator set, Figure 5, is coupled to a 30 000 lb/h boost fired boiler Figure 6. This project shows an overall installation cost of £2.2m against savings on a 1987 basis of £440K. However, it is worth noting that the installation cost was fixed and largely payable through the contract period, (July 1987 to September 1988), against work done, whilst if the anticipated level of performance is achieved, due to rising electricity prices and reducing fuel cost the saving could increase dramatically over the latter half of 1988.

Last, but (certainly based on USA experience) not least, is the Combined Cycle system as indicated in Figure 1(e). In its most common form waste heat recovery steam from the exhaust of a gas turbine is fed to a steam turbine which for best operational efficiency should be of the back pressure type. Fixed H/P ratios variable between 1.5 : 1 and 3.5 : 1 would be typical with a back pressure turbine but for ratios variable between 0 : 1 and 3 : 1 a steam turbine with a condensing exhaust is required. Both cases incorporating supplementary firing of the exhaust gas boilers, without which the upper limits would be around 1.5 : 1 fixed and 1.2 : 1 variable, respectively. Sometimes two gas turbines are coupled with one steam turbine but this does not affect the above.

The combined cycle extends the gas turbine capability to lower H/P ratios than if operating alone and can also provide flexibility, important if meeting thermal loads incorporating a large annual environmental element, whether this be for heating in winter or absorption chiller air conditioning, in the summer. Unfortunately, it is an expensive system and tends to be economic only at larger sizes, unless some retrofit is involved, for example, a gas turbine installed to replace the standard force-draught fan of a large fired boiler already serving steam turbines.

Economics

The benefits arising from energy conservation whether from cogeneration or other actions are well known and clearly indicated in Figure 7, however in practice, as always, there are some complications. The five major factors affecting the economics of cogeneration systems are:-

(a) The increase in overall conversion efficiency achieved by the cogeneration plant as compared with that of separate plant, see Figure 8

Here the efficiency of the on-site separate thermal output producer will be comparable with that of the cogeneration plant but the separate system overall efficiency will be lowered by the 30% to 35% achieved by a utility power station. Seen by the user as the high cost of bought-in electricity. It is also worth noting that the lower the heat to power ratio of the operational demands the lower is the separate plant overall efficiency

(b) The difference in price between the bought-in cost of electricity and the fuel used by the cogeneration system. Again the lower the H/P ratio of the demands the greater the effect of this factor on economic performance to the advantage of the cogeneration system

(c) The difference in price between the cost of the fuels used by the conventional boilers and the cogeneration system. The effect of this increases with the ratio of the heat to power demands

(d) The difference in manning and maintenance cost of the cogeneration and on-site separate plant

(e) The difference in capital cost of the cogeneration and the on-site separate plant.

Figure 9 indicates the average changes in energy costs for large industrial consumers taken from the D of E publication 'Energy Trends'; note the seasonal nature of electricity costs, between 1981 and the end of 1987, whilst Table 1 shows similar information on the basis of what a smaller industrial user could typically expect to pay for his energy supplies, as indicated by current prices published by The Energy Information Centre at that time.

There is a variance between the above for 1986 with the Table 1 figures being higher for coal and lower for gas than those plotted in Figure 9. This probably reflects the volatility of the market place at that time and the difficulty of obtaining truly typical costs in a very competitive situation, which is still ongoing, and prone to local distortions for all kinds of reasons.

Using the figures recorded in Table 1, and assuming an electrical output of around 5 MW, Table 2 computes the effects of cycle efficiency and relative energy costs for a number of systems. It also indicates the operating cost of the cogeneration and separate plant for the years 1984 (peak energy cost), 1986 (typical of today) and a predicted logical future when fuel prices relate to fuel quality, ie inversely to the ease of using and lack of environmental effect.

It must be recognised that the relative costs as calculated are at best only indicative since in practice:-

(a) The heat and power demands on the plant will vary

(b) The cycle efficiency of all plants varies with changes in heat and power output

(c) Interaction of electricity tariffs with load demand must be taken into account also the extent of electrical cost that is non-avoidable

(d) The performance of one gas turbine or reciprocating engine etc to another as power producers are different, as is the effect they and other items of equipment have on system characteristics and these will differ again at both design and part load conditions

(e) Operating and maintenance costs of course vary from one type of equipment and system to the next, but this is far from the whole story as they can also vary considerably from one installation to the next, sometimes for reasons not strictly within the control of the plant supplier

(f) Last but not least are 'peculiar', but no less real, special factors that may apply in particular circumstances - for instance, in Table 2 a dual fuel reciprocating engine system is compared with a gas turbine system using gas purchased at the same price. However, in line with British Gas's alternative fuel pricing policy you can today obtain gas for the former at a cheaper rate than the latter, since larger dual fuel engines can be operated satisfactorily on residual fuel oil varying from 960 to 4400 Redwood secs, dependent on the actual engine selected, whereas industrial sized gas turbines require distillate oil if gas is not available.

The Future

.1 Technical Developments

One of the most significant recent developments is the steam injection gas turbine cycle. This can provide gas turbines with the flexibility to operate from a normal 4 : 1 heat to power ratio, to one with full steam injection of 0 : 1, see Figure 10, where the power can in fact be increased by 60% (ie 0 : 1.6 ratio) with, at the same time, an increase in the efficiency of conversion to power of 18% (ie 41% rather than 35%). Theoretically an improvement in the order of 30% is possible in efficiency, hence there is still room for further improvement. These characteristics fit well large commercial buildings with significant computer facilities and light process industries using refrigeration techniques, as with both, electrical load often increases in summer periods when there is a reduced call for heat.

Boost firing the exhaust gas of reciprocating engines which provides a similar flexibility to the gas turbine system with supplementary firing and steam injection, has now been demonstrated commercially, however, there is still considerable development potential as regards detailed equipment improvement and system integration. For example, modification to the air fuel control on dual fuel engines, Figure 11 shows the system used on a Pielstick PC 2.3 engine. If the air bypass line discharged into the exhaust instead of being returned to the turbo-charger inlet it would increase exhaust gas mass flow and oxygen level to allow more and easier boost firing.

However, the most pressing need for reciprocating engine systems is to match the availability of gas turbines. Achieving this will depend upon the readiness of engine manufacturers, or others to set up on a 'national'/'international' scale 'maintenance contract'/'service organisations' such that on annual shutdown a team of men with the appropriate 'exchange' sub-assemblies and other items are on site ready to strip, rebuild and put the unit back into operation in the minimum time.

The future for fired boilers and steam turbines probably in the longer term lies with burning low grade fuels and operating at higher pressures and temperatures to reduce heat to power ratios. However, in the shorter term whilst gas and oil remain relatively cheap there could be a nitch for low cost, easily resitable, high pressure boiler package

complete with all necessary auxiliaries, and a similar arrangement of turbine. Providing the latter should be no problem whilst one firm is already 85% down the develoment path with the former. Availability of the above would reduce the lead time on installations from years to months, halve the project cost overall and totally transform the economic viability of steam turbine systems.

Potential

In 1986 the Department of Energy published a report 'Combined Heat and Power and Electricity Generation in British Industry 1983-1988' which examined the potential for Cogeneration in the traditional user industries. Pre-privatisation this indicated an overall reduction in industrial electricity production arising from the decommissioning of old oversize boiler/steam turbine plants but at the same time a switch to gas turbine and reciprocating engine systems such that 50% of the total predicted installation of 380 MWe of new equipment would be of this type. The latter has not yet happened but it is more likely that the timescale was wrong, rather than the prognosis itself. At the same time as the above, another report from a consultant was commissioned by the D of E to assess CHP (cogen) potential in non-traditional user industries, which really means those whose thermal demand is too small or inconsistent to be met by the traditional boiler/steam turbine system. This Report is still not published (Nov 1988) but it is believed that when originally offered in 1986 the estimated potential, based on a 5-year acceptable payback, was around 1200 MWe. Since then this Report has been under review and it is believed when ultimately published it will indicate a 200 to 300 MWe potential.

Government imposed price increases for electricity, some cynics suggest to fatten the industry up for privatisation, have improved the economics of cogeneration. However, that privatisation will increase cogeneration usage is not certain because, whilst the UK's electricity demand is expanding, it is not doing so rapidy and for sure it will not expand infinitely. Therefore under a privatised scenario the new generators that privatisation is aimed at encouraging are going to impinge not only on the National Power and Powergen Companies but also on the distribution boards who could be adversely affected should private generating companies, utilising heat demands for cogeneration, contract to supply prime demand industrial consumers direct. Then again, a number of boards are clearly indicating an intention themselves to generate 10% to 15% of their electricity sales and a private board may be more aggressively protective of its own generation operation than the ESI has been for many years. The rules of regulation will hold the key.

The terms of regulation will be critical for the larger electrical generation/cogeneration schemes, however they are unlikely to seriously affect the smaller, perhaps less than 10 MWe ones, where virtually all the power is generated for self use on an industrial or commercial site, (what the Americans call

'Bypass Meter' schemes). These currently are, and may well remain, the most economically advantageous and hence be the growth area for the forseeable future.

Conclusions

The Author believes that gas turbine plants with appropriate suplementary firing and/or steam injection will be predominant where the size of scheme and availability of reasonably priced natural gas allows; fired boilers and steam turbines, where low grade, low cost waste fuels are available and reciprocating engine systems using residual heavy fuel oil, where neither waste fuel nor low cost natural gas is available.

Based on sound economic sense and through the more efficient use of fuels, reduced environmental damage and the conservation of invaluable fossil resources it may be confidently anticipated that cogeneration will be a dynamic factor in working and possibly everyday life for the next 10, 20, 30, 40 ..? years.

The Author wishes to thank the Partners and Colleagues in McLellan and Partners Ltd for their help in preparing the paper, and NEI, Cyanamid and others for making available photographs and other material.

Fred Nash, CEng, FIMechE, FInstE, has been involved with industrial power generation and services for over 25 years, the last eight of which as Manager Special Projects Group with NEI-APE Ltd. In that capacity he led the development of the engine/boost fired boiler cogeneration system and was responsible for the system design of its first commercial application at Cyanamid UK.

On 1 October 1988 he joined Consultants, McLellan and Partners Ltd, West Byfleet, Surrey as Group Director, Power, Energy and Utilities.

		#1973	1981	1983	3rd Quarter 1984	May 1986
FUEL OIL	£ per tonne (Includes Tax)	12.8	108.2	125.9	151	60
	p per therm	3.11	26.65	31.0	37.2	16.3
Tax:	£ per tonne	+2.25	+8.0	+8.0	+8.0	+8.0
COAL	£ per tonne	8.9	39.9	49.6	49.8	55
	p per therm	3.4	15.52	19.07	19.1	22
Tax:		None	None	None	None	None
ELECTRICITY	p/kWh	0.74	2.71	2.94	2.69	3.0
	p per therm	21.68	79.29	85.09	77.85	88.9
GAS	p per therm	3.07	21.59	24.06	26.27	21.0*
Tax:		None	None	None	None	None
Ratio of Cost:						
	Elect/oil	6.97	2.97	2.74	2.09	5.5
	Elect/coal	6.38	5.11	4.45	4.10	4.1
	Elect/gas	7.06	3.67	3.53	2.96	4.2

1. All costs per therm refer to therms net CV.
2. Interruptible supply *. Where gas is in a non-competitive situation costs are approx 33p/therm (Gross) 36.6p/therm (Net)

Table 1 UK Energy Costs

CHP SYSTEM	HEAT/POWER RATIO	SYSTEM EFFICIENCY	FUEL USED	DECEMBER 1984		MAY 1986		FUTURE		RELATIVE COST CHP PLANT
				FUEL COST INDEX (ELECT 4)	RELATIVE OPERATING COSTS CHP BASIC 1	FUEL COST INDEX (ELECT 4.1)	RELATIVE OPERATING COSTS CHP BASIC 3	FUEL COST INDEX (ELECT 5)	RELATIVE OPERATING COSTS CHP BASIC 2	
Steam Boiler/ Turbine	8/1	84%	Coal	1	0.50	1 (HFO) = 0.74	0.94 (0.70)	1	0.55	2.5
Diesel Engine/ Boost Fired Boiler	3.6/1	84%	Heavy Fuel	1.8	0.83	0.74	0.55	1.2	0.57	1
Dual Fuel Eng/ Boost Fired Boiler	3.6/1	86%	Diesel (8%) N.G.	2.4 1.3	0.61	1.25 0.95	0.70	1.7 1.5	0.70	1.3
Gas Turbine/ Fired W.H.R. Boiler	2/1	79%	Natural Gas	1.3	0.59	0.95	0.61	1.5	0.66	1
Dual Fuel Eng/ Fired W.H.R. Boiler	2/1	81%	Diesel (8%) N.G.	2.4 1.3	0.60	1.25 0.95	0.73	1.7 1.5	0.64	1.2

Basic Energy Provision - Purchased Electricity + Heat from Low Pressure Boilers
Based on information from D of E Energy Trends Dec '84, i.e. Elect 2.7p/kWh, Coal £50/t, HFO £151/t, Gas 26.3p/therm.

1. Basic Operating Cost Dec '84 based on Electricity Cost Index 4 and HFO used in L.P. Boilers
2. "   "   "   " Future   "   "   "   " Index 5 " Gas "   "   "   "
3. "   "   "   " May '86 "   "   "   " Index 4 " HFO "   "   "   "

Table 2 Economic Comparison of Cogenerating Systems

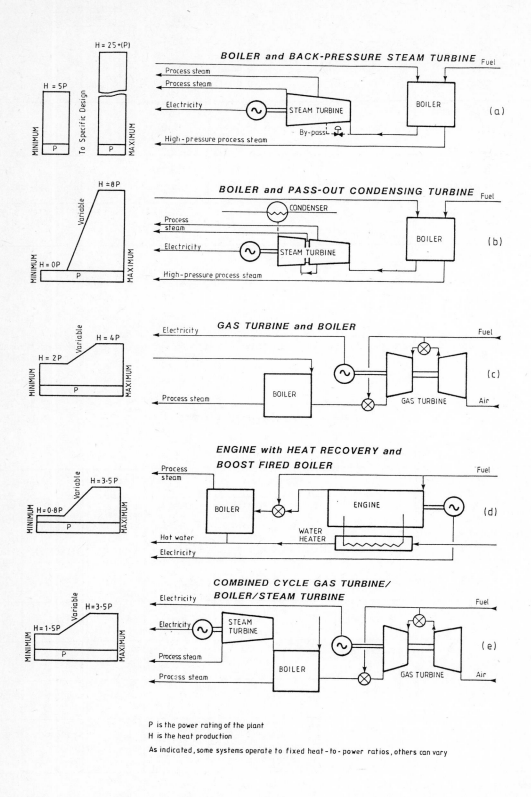

P is the power rating of the plant
H is the heat production
As indicated, some systems operate to fixed heat-to-power ratios, others can vary

Fig 1   Types of co-generation systems

Fig 2   Industrial gas turbine installation

Fig 3   Typical spark ignition engine (Micro) installation

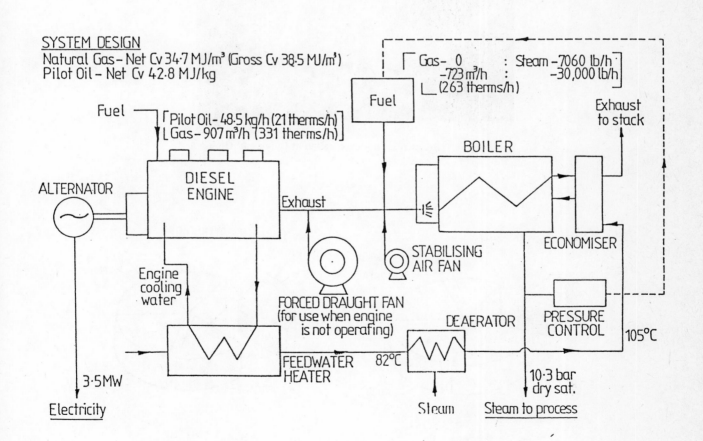

Fig 4   Diagrammatic representation of dual fuel engine system installed at
         Cyanamid

Fig 5   Dual fuel engine installed at Cyanamid UK

Fig 6   Boost fired boiler installed at Cyanamid UK

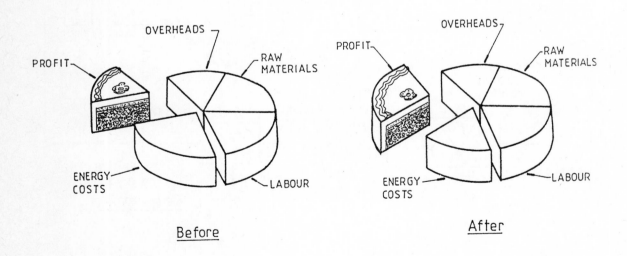

Fig 7   Economic benefits of energy conservation

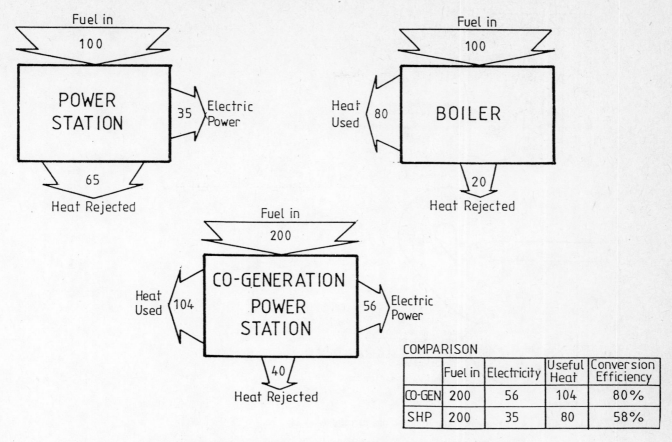

COMPARISON	Fuel in	Electricity	Useful Heat	Conversion Efficiency
CO-GEN	200	56	104	80%
SHP	200	35	80	58%

Fig 8   Energy comparison: standard (SHP) and co-generation (CO-GEN)

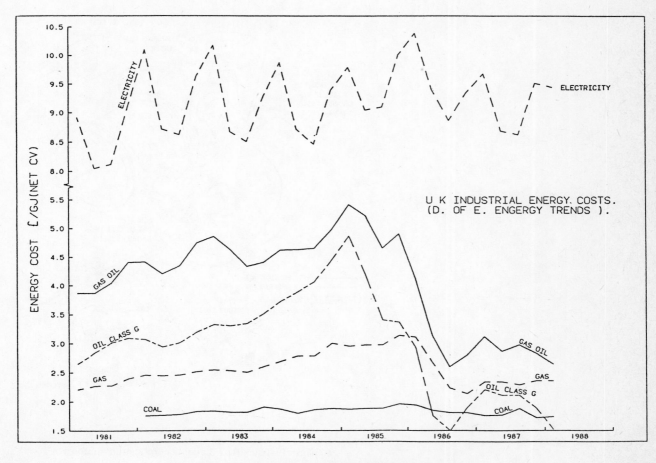

Fig 9   Historic comparison of UK energy costs

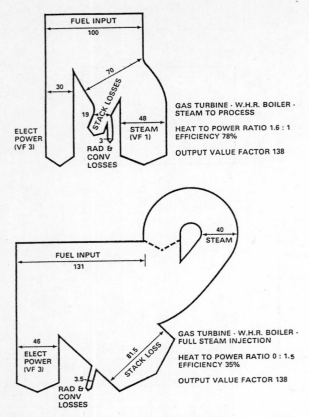

GAS TURBINE · W.H.R. BOILER ·
STEAM TO PROCESS

HEAT TO POWER RATIO 1.6 : 1
EFFICIENCY 78%

OUTPUT VALUE FACTOR 138

GAS TURBINE · W.H.R. BOILER ·
FULL STEAM INJECTION

HEAT TO POWER RATIO 0 : 1.5
EFFICIENCY 35%

OUTPUT VALUE FACTOR 138

Fig 10   Sankey diagram of typical steam injected gas turbine

AIR-FUEL RATIO CONTROL SYSTEM

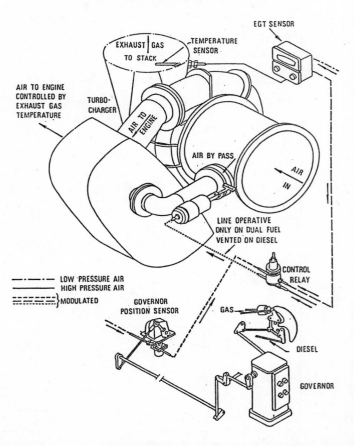

Fig 11   Pielstick PC2.3 engine combustion air control

Installation, commissioning, and hand-over of large diesel plant

J H BLOWES, CEng, FIMarE, MIMechE, MIDGTE
Project Manager (Special Projects), Mirrlees Blackstone (Stockport) Limited

SYNOPSIS

Installation and commissioning of large diesel plant has become more onerous in recent years due to the increasing complexity and ability of systems, together with the increasing demands of Quality Assurance, which in its own right serves to ensure that plant is designed, manufactured, installed and commissioned to specification. The paper forms an overview of the subject and attempts to touch on the full range of requirements, allowing then a choice to be developed to suit any particular application.

1. INTRODUCTION

Installation, commissioning and handover of diesel plant is discussed, with particular emphasis on preparatory work, leading to successful completion on time, within budget and to specification.

The methods may be applied to any prime mover, provided that the complexity of installation and commissioning is geared to individual requirements, associated with its duty.

For example, due to its complexity, plant which will serve as standby to Nuclear power generation, tends to require a greater intensity of pre-testing and a higher level of Quality Assurance than for marine propulsion or routine industrial duties.

2. HANDOVER

Prior to proceeding further with technical aspects, commercial influences need to be considered.

Cost, whether to the contractor or the purchaser, is a very significant governing factor and will always be hovering in the background when engineers are making decisions to ensure that the plant meets all relevant specifications.

The main contractor will hand over "the works" to the purchaser when he has proven that it performs to specification, although the subcontractor, having a shorter programme will naturally wish to achieve commercial acceptance at an earlier stage.

It is well worthwhile setting check points where actual costs versus completion to specification are routinely monitored. These points would be set when significant portions of plant are invoiced by the subcontractor or on a periodic basis.

The subcontractor must therefore be made fully aware of his responsibilities and the method devised for him to prove compliance agreed, before he commences.

Whilst the effectiveness of Quality Assurance (QA) must not be impaired by commercial constraints, it does need to be fully complied with if plant handed over is to be within specification.

Linking QA and commercial interests is therefore beneficial.

A package of work will be technically acceptable if the associated QA documentation is fully signed off by the engineer. Handover or even a stage payment could be permitted, against the issue of QA documentation or a QA certificate of completion.

With todays ever increasing QA requirements this approach can provide the added control needed in the short term by a main contractor, instead of his pursuing minor contractual breaches by more traditionally recognised methods.

As we have shown, handover and acceptance is applicable to all defined stages of a project and therefore we shall see it appear a number of times under subsequent headings.

3. COMPLEXITY OF TESTING

Before the fine detail of installation and commissioning or its complexity, is considered, we need to review broader aspects:-

(a) The duty of the plant, including adverse conditions, parameters to be proven and methods of simulation during testing.

(b) If the plant is duplicated, which "type" tests will be allowed.

(c) Consider the need for specialist services.

(d) Determine documentation requirements and methods of formal approval.

(e) Consider any design changes which are necessary to aid installation and commissioning.

Dealing with each heading in turn:-

(a) Duty and Simulation

The duty will already have been defined, although extremes of load or site conditions may not.

We should certainly consider:-

(i) Steady state and step loads.

Use of load banks to provide flexibility during commissioning provided that they simulate the service load.

Decide on the type of test instrumentation to be used and the speed at which results and the analysis need to be produced.

For example, if the results of one test need to be analysed by a lengthy method prior to the next test beginning, then the prime mover and part of the team may frequently be idle.

(ii) Noise.

Modern highly rated plant often produces noise levels which make the whole building an "ear protection area" and although a degree of silencing is employed internally, silencing is targeted at reducing the noise outside the building, to an acceptable level, for environmental reasons.

No simulation will of course be necessary here, although the plant should be in its completed state, prior to the measurements being carried out.

(iii) Vibration.

The effect of one item of plant, normally the prime mover on others-control equipment in particular, or outside influences including earth tremors or earthquakes.(Seismic considerations)

Looking a little more closely at vibration; make use of shake table tests early in the manufacturing programme or accept the manufacturers assurances if the plant is of an identical design with long term proven reliability.

When it comes to site testing, possible vibration levels under abnormal service conditions can often be carefully induced, for the purpose of monitoring its effect on the installation "as built". For example, the prime mover can be operated at various speeds and if necessary in the case of a diesel engine, with a degree of imbalance between the load taken by each cylinder.

Whilst sophisticated electronic recording equipment is necessary, a high percentage of problem areas can be identified initially by simple observation, prior to the sophisticated equipment being brought into play.

A number of "Seismic" excitable pipe runs could be identified visually following a movement induced with the hand as the frequencies which give rise to concern are less than 41 cycles/second and by the nature of such a low frequency, movements are clearly visible.

Having said this however, uncharacteristic prime mover torsional vibrations, which can cause disastrous failures without warning, cannot be observed without electronic measuring equipment. A "type" test is often required to support calculation.

Having identified the more obvious pipe work vibrational problems by simple methods, the more sophisticated approach can be commenced before the plant becomes operational, provided that the pipework contains the working fluid.

Vibration can be induced by application of a small impact. Analysis of the resulting frequencies and amplitudes will then assist in determining the effect of greater movements and high stress areas.

The position of additional pipework support may also be determined quite easily from the same analytical methods.

It should be remembered that although a particular item of plant may not be essential to operation in the defined emergency conditions, it may still require seismic qualification.

Damage can quite easily be caused if non essential plant fails; the overhead crane falling on essential plant, for example.

(iv) High wind loading is difficult to simulate although calculations tend to be reasonably accurate, thus a few assumptions are necessary.

It may be worthwhile considering the consequential damage of high winds, the piece of steel corrugated roofing material which blocks an air filter, for example.

(v) The temperate climate of the UK may relate to cold rather than hot site conditions, although tests obviously need be carried out to demonstrate capability under both extremes.

High temperature can be simulated by reducing cooling efficiency and low only by testing in cold weather or by producing a cold environment around a particular item of plant.

High oil viscosity in a gearbox, brittle fracture of a drive belt, freezing air in the pneumatic control system and the ability of the plant to start, following long term standing during a cold period may all need to be proven prior to handover.

(vi) If the fire fighting equipment is of the deluge type and the prime mover is to carry out its duty regardless of gallons of water being sprayed on it then the actual service conditions would seem to be the only answer.

A balance between simulating adverse conditions on site and support by calculation is essential, as damaged caused by overcooling, overheating, and drenching could quickly outweigh the costs of replacement, not to mention unacceptable programme delays.

b) **Adverse Conditions**

These will vary considerably according to the duty of the plant. Some examples may be:-

Reduced voltage, high or low operating temperatures, high altitude, high humidity, corrosive atmosphere, long periods of standby without operation, drastic load changes due to mining shovels cutting into earth, or ships ploughing into a rough sea.

(c) **Type Tests**

These may include:-

(i) Shaker table tests as already mentioned.

(ii) Alternator and diesel coupled together with its auxiliary equipment, at the manufacturer's works, to serve as a combined test.

(iii) Torsiograph tests as mentioned earlier.

(iv) Sub-zero starting of any chosen item of plant.

(d) **Specialist Services**

Specialists are those who deal with a particular aspect routinely and therefore will be more able to advise or carry out installation and commissioning on behalf of a contractor.

Each subcontractor should be considered as a specialist who will provide plant installation procedures around a skeleton format, pertinent to his product.

Other specialists may be employed to prove a particular aspect of the design and demonstrate the effectiveness of their calculations on site.

Seismic qualification is a typical example, exhaust gas analysis, radiography of welds or recording of data are others.

(e) **Document Approval**

The whole subject will be governed by the customer's requirements or needs:-

Statutory authority, private power generation or marine propulsion are examples of different needs.

To satisfy a government body that the documentation meets safety requirements of a Nuclear installation is probably the most severe, with QA to BS 5882. This compared to installing and commissioning plant to drive a water pump in a remote desert site is perhaps at the other end of the scale.

It will help if the documentation is written to cater for:-

Non-compliances, action required and defect clearance as work proceeds, with carry over of outstanding actions to the next stage:-

Typical stages may well be:-

(i)   Delivery to site

(ii)   Installation

(iii)   Point to point cable or pneumatic pipework route checks

(iv)   Instrument calibration

(v)   Flow of fluids and electricity

(vi)   Operation of individual systems.

(vii)   Operation and proving the plant as a whole

(viii) Handover

A portion of the documentation will need to be retained as lifetime records, both to trouble shoot in-service problems and also for routine comparison with future monitoring to determine if changes have occurred whilst the plant is in service.

It should also be determined if the results will be approved by one authorised engineer or by an expert committee?

(f)   Design Changes

Design must not only concern itself with the service duty of the plant, but also the installation and commissioning.

Lifting and securing heavy plant requires expertise and positive thought by the designer.

eg.

A 16ton silencer, could not be lifted from the delivery vehicle, rotated from the horizontal position to vertical and temporarily secured without detailed design consideration.

The 100ton prime mover will need pulling points within the building to winch it into position.

In an ideal world, the designer will have designed the holes in auxiliary base plates to be accessible for the drilling machine to drill foundations without the plant needing to be moved again to insert the holding down bolts.

On the commissioning front, very considerable time may be saved if test equipment is of the "plug in type".

The designer could provide approved jack plug sockets, rather than the electrical commissioning engineer having to connect his monitoring equipment into existing circuitry and then prove that he has not affected the operation of the plant following its removal.

Such sockets would then be used by the purchaser repeatedly, for plant monitoring, on a routine basis.

4. INSTALLATION

(a) Organisation

Even if the QA level is not sufficiently high to call for a statement on how the site is to be organised, a document showing the organisational structure with detailed responsibilities of individuals should be produced.

(b) Site Layout

If there is a choice, the storage area, offices, changing rooms etc should be close together.

Those concerned must have easy access to drawings, procedures and standards, without incurring excessive "walking time".

The advantages of storing tools close to the working area must be considered in relation to the increased security of them being returned to a main store each night.

(c) Safety and Industrial Relations

Safety and Industrial relations so often go hand in hand, and both are extremely important subjects in their own right.

Under the heading of "The Route to Success" treat Safety and Industrial Relations, with the respect which they both deserve.

Handled on a low priority basis, both will cost dearly.

Ensure that the site manager and his deputy are fully versed in statutory requirements as well as other essential customs and practices.

Routinely provide information to the workforce and hold regular meetings to assess present difficulties and those anticipated in the next package of work.

(d) Training

It may be economic for an existing work force to carry out semi-specialised work, given training or re-training, although the work needs to be associated with their own recognised trades,

For example:-

One team may be quite capable of installing copper control piping, and only be in need of short term training to bring them to the standard required to install stainless steel pipework.

The foregoing tends to relate to specialised off-site training, although on the job training on a "father to son" basis is nearly always effective.

Correctly chosen, one experienced and one less experienced engineer working together will often produce two experienced men who can carry out the same task in separate locations.

(e) Installation Documentation

Installation Documentation is needed to provide information and to show when work has been completed to specification as well as serving as a long term historic record.

Taking the most obvious installation stages in turn:-

Prior to work commencing, the informative documentation must be in place.

This includes:-

(i) Welder approval certificates

(ii) Lifting equipment register

(iii) Drawings and drawing register

(iv) Procedures

(v) Standards

(vi) QA Programme

The records, commencing with the installation checksheets will commence when the first item of plant arrives at site and will record defects arising from the journey, in addition to the carry over of defects from the factory release certificate.

The factory release certificate (often a form of handover) will only relate to the higher QA levels, although whilst not contractually essential, it and other QA documentation in a simple form, as mentioned earlier can be very useful.

It is normally easier to monitor plant during installation if one check sheet is used for each individual item of plant.

These sheets will then remain available through commissioning to provide a recent history and will form a part of the documentation handed over to the purchaser at the end of the day, who will retain them as a lifetime record.

Other records may include a "Modification Register" to monitor all major or minor changes to specification, or perhaps an "Engineering Query Register" which will monitor site queries on engineering matters with head office replies.

5. COMMISSIONING

As mentioned earlier, commissioning is the stage where electricity and fluids flow although "pre-commissioning" is often included under the same subject heading.

A more specialised team of operators or commissioning engineers need to be employed.

They will authorise filling the systems with oil and water followed by energising the plant.

The commissioning team should ideally be involved with pre-commissioning and post handover trials to provide continuity. Repeated learning curves by a succession of "new" engineers is expensive.

Keeping one large team with sufficient reserve to accommodate illness and holidays has proven more effective than duplicating teams and equipment.

In particular the learning curve through installation and commissioning the first set of equipment can be quite dramatic.

Using as an example, the learning curves of installing and commissioning four power stations for standby to Nuclear duty from 1983 to 1985; the workforce "booked" onto job numbers which assisted programming and budget predictions.

The periods taken to install and commission were:-

Power Station	Installation	Commissioning
A	100%	100%
B	81%	90%
C	79%	77%
D	71%	63%

Commissioning can be divided into three main areas:-

STAGE 1   Pre-commissioning

All instruments will be calibrated, either in situ or in the workshop.

Point to point cable and wiring checks will be made and control pipework will be point to point checked and leak tested.

The pipework subcontractor may be allowed to hand over his portion of the work following a low pressure flange joint leak test.

A form of handover will be noted here.

Commissioning will be allowed, provided that pre-commissioning defects not affecting commissioning are clear. The remaining defects being carried over, with the intention of clearance prior to client acceptance.

The commissioning engineer will need to approve filling of systems and will base his judgment on the documentation available which will include high pressure (hydraulic) pipework tests and pipework support checks.

Low pressure leak tests, perhaps using air up to 10 PSI are of particular value with lubricating oil pipework. Water leaks are of course not so bad but once oil is present then remedial action is much more expensive.

Concrete floors which could receive spillages, especially lubricating oil should have already been treated in advance of this stage.

STAGE 2   Commissioning

Each system will now be commissioned as far as possible in isolation.
Examples are:-

Water pump motors will have their insulation resistance measured and will be dried out, if necessary, followed by a motor directional check.

It is normal to circulate all fluids around their respective systems with some form of filter, whether it be the service filter and/or a strong wire mesh.

It is sound practice to circulate the systems bypassing the prime mover until the system has been shown to have reached the defined cleanliness standard.

The amount of debris collected will be evident from filter inspections.

Circulation also serves the purpose of allowing the pump to work and operate against a pressure head as a further precheck.

It is quite common practice for all welds to be hammered on the outside of the pipe to release any slag which may otherwise release during normal operation.

When circulating oil through filters it is preferable to operate the heaters, if fitted, as fine debris is filtered more easily at higher temperatures. Alternatively, the energy imparted by the oil pumping process may increase the temperature sufficiently.

A long term programming note is worthwhile here. Programme circulation of water from autumn onwards in climates which experience sub zero temperatures. Filling a water system in January is far too risky unless you can afford the luxury of a water tanker containing water and antifreeze solution to facilitate fill and drain down.

The last system to be operated will be the prime mover itself using all of the other systems for support.

The first objective will be to run and demonstrate safety devices.

The Prime mover is then loaded, electrically in the case of a power station or perhaps by rotation of the propeller with a small amount of pitch applied whilst moored, for a marine application.

The object here, is to operate at a slow speed and/or load and observe. By this approach there is a far better chance of avoiding a serious problem.

With confidence increased, apply the load in accordance with recommended running in procedures and demonstrate the more sophisticated safety devices as early as circumstances permit.

The load control should be sufficiently versatile to be shed immediately if the operator senses a problem. Good communication between the observers and load controller is essential.

Whilst the foregoing may appear to be over cautious, modern power plants are expensive and mistakes equally so.

The prime mover should be fully run-in, balanced and all alarms and safety devices demonstrated where possible in the true operating environment.

STAGE 3 Proving

It is now time to prove that the set can operate under the adverse conditions defined in the specification, although a reliability run is normally carried out first. Not only to build up confidence in the plant but also to iron out minor problems which may necessitate shutdowns during dynamic testing.

If the reliability run is contractual then a pre run would be carried out before the formal reliability trial.

It is normal to set-up recording instrumentation before the reliability trial to obtain provisional information and to use the operational time to set up the equipment.

It also serves as a reliability period for the instrumentation.

Determine which instrumentation cannot easily be replaced and provide a backup. These costs can be weighed against possible loss of programme time should one fail.

The formal results should be those which become lifetime records and indeed those which may be considered to be a "fingerprint", to be used at a later date for comparison when certain tests need to be repeated, i.e., following fitting of a new governor or after dismantling a major section of the plant.

This is where the "plug in" test facility mentioned earlier under the design heading, will be of value.

6.   POST HANDOVER PROVING

Conclusion of the foregoing tests is normally associated with handover from the main contractor to the client who will now wish to use the plant either commercially or to prove the remainder of his installation, using the recently handed over plant in its entirety.

Retaining the original team or working party here is of utmost importance, not forgetting also training of personnel who will operate and probably retest against the "fingerprint".

Defects not affecting commercial operation, should become "provisions" appended to the acceptance certificate and carried over into the warranty period, through which, further minor defects will be recorded and corrected.

BIBLIOGRAPHY

Commencing life in the industry as a diesel engine design engineer, the author has been actively involved in trouble shooting technical and commercial problems arising in the field for the majority of his career.

Together with his own and the company's overall increasing experience, he has been able to develop procedures to install and commission plant to current day requirements.

ACKNOWLEDGEMENTS

The author wishes to express his thanks to Mirrlees Blackstone (Stockport) Ltd for permission to publish the information contained in this paper.

The opinions expressed however, are attributable solely to the author.

Meeting the power requirements of an island community

K KIMSTRA, Dipl Ing
Engineering Manager, Stork-Werkspoor Diesel Projects, Amsterdam

1. SUMMARY

This paper deals with some aspects of the recent extension of the CARIBBEAN UTILITIES CO. diesel power station on Grand Cayman with 2 each 10.3 MWe units.

First a brief description is given of the size and duty of station.

Second, the recent extension with 2 x 10.3 MWe units will be described in some more detail.

Special attention will be given to the application of a so called power turbine in which part of the exhaust gases expand in a separate gas turbine which drives its' own generator; a practice which contributes to low fuel consumption per total kWh generated.

Attention will further be given to the cooling system and to the foundation of the engine and generator. It is also shown what potential the engines concerned have for waste heat recovery.

Finally, a few characteristical properties of large bore medium speed four stroke engines will be discussed which are interesting from the point of cost per kWh generated.

2. THE CUC GRAND CAYMAN DIESEL POWER STATION

The CUC Grand Cayman power station supplies electricity and water to all users on Grand Cayman Island in the Caribbean. Water is mainly produced with the use of heat taken from the exhaust gases of the diesel engines.

Installed power before the extension with 20.6 MWe was about 30 MW divided over smaller units than the ones recently installed. After the extension with these and a smaller unit and retirement of some obsolete power the installed capacity has risen to 55.1 MW with a firm capacity of 48 MW for a peakload of 35 MW and a minimum load of 21 MW.

This 21 MW load means that the station has usually enough load to have the 2 largest units running all the time at or near full load.

Figure 1 shows a cross-section on the new part of the station.

3. THE NEW 10.3 MWe DIESEL GENERATING UNITS

The new diesel engines model 8 TM 620 were built by Clark Kincaid under licence of Stork-Werkspoor Diesel of Holland.

Their main characteristics are:

Bore	620	mm
Stroke	660	mm
No. of Cylinders	8	
RPM	400	
BMEP incl. Power Turbine	20	Bar
BMEP (engine shaft power only)	19	Bar
Mean piston speed	9.4	m/s
Maximum combustion pressure	150	Bar

Figure 2 shows a cross-section of this engine.

This model of engine has been in production since 1975 and has been modernized at intervals to keep it up to date with present day technology.

The original design has a track record of over 60,000 hours per engine and modernisation of the model has been done in relatively small steps, each time after considerable testing on a full scale 6 cylinder test unit in the works in Amsterdam.

4. THE ENGINE AND POWER TURBINE COMBINATION

In modern large turbo-charged diesel engines a turbocharger does not need all the engines' exhaust gas for supplying the amount of air required in the upper load range.

The portion of gas the turbocharger does not require can be branched off from just upstream of the turbine and can be piped to a separate turbine. Through a reduction gear this turbine can be coupled to the engines' crankshaft or to a separate generator, the latter is the case in CUC. Figure 3 is a picture of the unit installed in the CUC station.

The turbine drives an asynchronous generator the terminals of which are connected - through a coupler - to the terminals of the diesel driven synchronous generator, see figures 4 and 5.

The operation of the turbine is controlled by 2 valves, turbine inlet valve A and bypass valve B.

At engine start both valves are closed and remain closed up until about 55% engine load.

When after starting the engine the exitation of the main generator is switched on, the turbo alternator - a squirrel cage machine - starts motoring its turbine and runs it up to a speed just under-synchronous with the main generator. It absorbs then about 50 kW.

When engine load has increased to 55% valve A is opened and the turbine speeds its' generator up from about 1% under-synchronous onto some 2% over-synchronous speed and starts generating power.

When the diesel engine has reached its full load of 10100 kW (9850 kW at generator terminals) the turbo generator generates 500 kWs/450 kWe, bringing the total output at 10600 kWs/10300 kWe at a specific fuel consumption which is about 4 g/kWhe lower than would be obtained with an engine equipped with a turbocharger having a turbine with larger flow area and lower exhaust manifold pressure.

Figure 6 shows curves of the specific fuel consumption over load for 3 engine arrangements:

1. the well matched and tuned standard diesel engine

2a. the engine with power turbine genset; the turbocharger matched accordingly

2b. the same arrangement as in 2a. but with the turbine inlet valve closed and the bypass valve open, turbine at rest (coupler open).

Where the fuel saving comes from is easily understood when one compares the P-V diagrams of the engines with and without power turbine.

Figure 7 shows these (ideal) P-V diagrams besides each other, left for the standard engine and right for the engine with power turbine. Consider first the standard engine and follow what happens to the 0.7 kg or 0.6 M of air required for one four stroke cycle in one cylinder.

The compressor sucks the air in at atmospheric pressure: line 1 → 2 in the diagram. Then follows compression to 3.3 bar/185°C (2 → 3), cooling to 50°C (3 → a) and pushing the air away into the engine (a → 4). The power done by the compressor on that $0.6m^3$ is represented by the area 1-2-3-4-1. The turbocharger turbine has done the work 5-6-7-1-5. The ratio between these two areas is equal to the thermodynamic efficiency of the turbocharger.

The engine receives power from the 3.3 bar air during the suction stroke a → b. Then it gives power to the air by compressing it from b → c, then again receives power when expanding after combustion from c → d followed by putting power in exhausting the cylinder e → f. The net power supplied to the crankshaft is represented by the area b-c-d-b plus the area a-b-e-f-a.

The triangle d-e-6-d represents the throttling loss occurring during the expansion of the gas from d to e when passing the exhaust valves. This is a pure loss. The loss turns into heat in the exhaust gas during the flow from cylinder to exhaust manifold, causing the starting point of the expansion in the turbine to lay right from the isentropic expansion line, in point 6 instead of in point 6.

The increase in turbocharger efficiency in the recent years has reduced the amount of turbine power required for achieving the 3.3 bar boostpressure. In the diagram this resulted in a downward movement of line 5-6, which increased the throttling although it increased the power from the scavenge loop e-f-a-b to the crankshaft. By applying a power turbine line 5-6 is lifted back into place as can be seen in the diagram at the right of Figure 7.

Here the turbocharger turbine has a smaller flow area, causing higher exhaust manifold pressure but needing only part of the exhaust gas for driving the same compressor with the same power as the other turbine did. The remainder of the gas is fed into the power turbine, at the same high exhaust manifold pressure. The power of these two turbines together is represented by the area 5-6-7-1-5 of which 5-6-(6)-(5)-5 is that of the power turbine. The engine looses the power e-d-(d)-(e) from its positive scavenge loop. The difference between 5-6-(6)-(5)-5 and e-f-(f)-(e)-e is the net gain in power. To compensate for the slightly higher thermal loading of the engine caused by the reduction in scavenge ratio, the engine rating is reduced by the power turbine output, leaving the total output unchanged compared to the standard engine. The net result is a reduction of specific fuel consumption of 4 to 5 grams per kWh.

5. ECONOMICS OF THE POWER TURBINE

The extra cost of the installed Power Turbine of the type concerned is in the order of $200,000.

Assume:

- running hours engine per year	6500
- running hours power turbine per year	6500
- load factor, percent	75
- cost of maintenance of turbine set $/kW/year $	20
- depreciation time of the turbine set, years	15
- interest rate, percent	10

Then it follows that:

- kWh generated per year in millions   50.2
- litres of .85 s.g. fuel saved,
                         in thousands   236
- annuity, percent   13.15
- annuity, $ 26,300
- maintenance cost, $ 11,000
- total cost $ 37,300

Break-even between costs and savings is reached at a fuel price of $0.158 per litre. At a fuel price of, for instance, $0.30 per litre annual savings after annuity and maintenance costs are paid are $33,512 or 17% of the purchase price (after annuity and other cost.)

From the above it can easily be calculated which the savings are at other fuel prices load factors, interest rates, etc.

6. THE ENGINE FOUNDATION

Each diesel engine together with its generator is mounted on a concrete block which on its turn is supported on steel springs, see Figure 8.

Supporting the concrete foundation block on steel springs has a number of advantages over stiff supporting. Firstly, the amount of vibration carried into the soil and through the soil into the powerhouse building and possibly also into adjacent buildings is negligible. Secondly, the total amount of concrete required to achieve a given calculated level of vibrations transmitted into the soil is considerably less, the difference often pays for the springs. Thirdly, the vibrating system is well defined and permits to calculate vibration levels with great accuracy, much better than with stiff foundations.

On the concrete foundation block sit 2 heavy cast iron girders, grouted with about 1 inch epoxy resin. The stiff girders spread the weight and the periodic forces from the engine evenly over the resin. Between the engines and the cast iron girders there are chocks which permit future alignment correction if such might be necessary. The anchor bolts are hydraulically tightened studbolts which reach from the top of the engine feet down to below the foundation block, putting everything under compressive stress.

Since its introduction in 1982 this design of connection between engine and foundation has been free from the troubles of concrete and grouting failures which plagued earlier designs of attachment of the engine to the block.

7. ENGINE COOLING

All engine systems have radiator cooling. Radiators absorb a little more power than raw water cooling pumps would do. Absorbed power for radiators is xx kW for cooling water and lube-oil, yy kW for charge air cooling whereas raw waterpumps for these systems would have needed about xx kW. The lower outage time and lower maintenance cost of the radiator solution however justify this choice.

6. WASTE HEAT POTENTIAL

The exhaust gas temperature of modern turbocharged medium speed diesel engines is almost independent of load. This means that also at part load where the bulk of the running hours are usually made a considerable percentage of the fuel heat is available at a usable temperature level.

Figure 9 shows the heat flows in the 8 TM 620 engine as a function of generator load.

Figure 10 shows the useful waste heat of exhaust gas, jacket water and charge air as a percentage of the generator load over the 25 to 100% generator load range. From this graph it can be seen, that if exhaust gas is cooled to 160°C one gets about .4 kWh heat as by-product from every kWe generated. Would also the heat of jacket water be recovered, the recovered heat would grow to around .55 kW per kWhe generated. Would in the engine load much of the time be above the 70% mark, then it would also be useful to recover part of the charge air heat bringing the total heat recovered at about .6 kWh per kWhe generated. In the upper load range the recoverable heat in the exhaust gas of the engine with power turbine is marginally higher than in the engine without power turbine. Although the latter has a higher massflow it has a lower exhaust temperature.

7. THE ECONOMICS OF LARGE BORE MEDIUM SPEED ENGINES WITH LIMITED NUMBER OF ENGINES

If for a given project one has to choose between 2 engine models of the same power but with different cylinder bore and with different number of cylinders, then, assuming the engines are of comparable quality of design, workmanship and technological level there are some interesting aspects to be looked at.

They are:

- Specific fuel consumption
- availability
- capital cost

We will look at each of these aspects separately.

Specific fuel consumption. Engines of comparable level of design but with different cylinder dimensions are found to have usually very much the same mean piston speeds. This means also that flow speeds in gas passages are very much the same. Reynolds numbers of gasflow are therefore smaller in the bigger engine and consequently also the flow friction losses. Comparable rules of scale apply for bearing friction, piston ring friction and other scale-sensitive phenomena. Many of these effects are not linear with engine size and are difficult to quantify. The book Internal Combustion Engines by C.F. Taylor and E.S. Taylor deals with these problems in detail.

We made a simple approach by comparing the specific fuel consumptions of a considerable number of comparable engines of different cylinder size it was found that a 50% increase in engine linear dimensions went along with about 10 grams per kWh lower specific fuel consumption. When the cylinder bore is taken as the characteristical linear dimension of the engine the effect of size on specific fuel consumption can reasonably well be approached by the formula

$$BSFC = C - 26 \times lnD \quad (BSFC \text{ in } g/kWk, D \text{ in } mm)$$

in which C is a constant which represents the technological level of the engine design.

Engine availability. Every year the Institution of Diesel and Gas Turbine Engineers publishes in their Annual Cost and Operational Report a break-down of causes of enforced engine stoppages. The ratio between cylinder related defects such as injector pipe failures, fuel pump failures, connecting rod bearing failures and not-cylinder related failures such as governor, turbocharger, gear train is always the same 2 to 1, which means that one is better off with the big bore unit with few cylinders than with the smaller bore unit with, say, double the number of cylinders as the smaller bore unit. Also the effect of cylinder size on availability can be numerically approached by making a number of assumptions regarding hours lost per defect, etc. Details of this approach were published in the June 1987 issue of our Company magazine SWDIESEL REVIEW. Working along these lines and for a given set of conditions one finds for an 8 cylinder unit an average availability of 7400 hours and for a 16 cylinder unit 6600 hours out of 8760 hours in a year, all relevant conditions being the same.

Capital cost. Weight and manufacturing cost per kWh power output of medium speed diesel engines increases roughly proportionally with cylinder dimensions. Investment per kW for 600 mm bore units would be about 10% more than for 400 mm bore units. Comparing 2 diesel power station designs capable of the same kWh output per year, the one with 8 cylinder large bore engines would require less units than a station with 18 cylinder units of the same unit rating, the ratio between the number of units being the inverse of the ratio of the availabilities of 8 cylinder units and 18 cylinder units. Let us see how this works out on kWh cost for a station producing 200 GWh per year.

We assume four engines, each producing 50 GWh per year. Four 8 cylinder units of 10 MW each, running 7400 hours would have to run at an average load of 77%.

Alternatively we look at four 18 cylinder units of 10 MW each, which with two thirds of the bore of the 8 cylinder units but the same bmep and piston speed also produce 10 MW per unit. Because of their higher number of cylinders these engines would under the same circumstances run about 6500 hours per year, and would produce 43.9 GWh per year at the same 77% average load. A total of 27.7 GWh would have to be purchased from other sources, assume from similar machinery. This could be translated in the requirement that not 40 MW capacity but 50/43.9 x 40 = 45.6 MW capacity should have been installed.

Assuming an investment cost of $600/kW for the 8 cylinder units and $525 for the 18 cylinder units, the difference in annual capital cost between the two cases would be $8000 in favour of 45.6 MW 18 cylinder capacity.

The specific fuel consumption of the 18 cylinders would however be 10 grams per kWh higher, which at a fuel price of $0.15 per litre would cost and extra $350,000.

Although in every real case the figures will differ from this example, the more fuel-economical large bore units will almost invariably generate cheaper kWh.

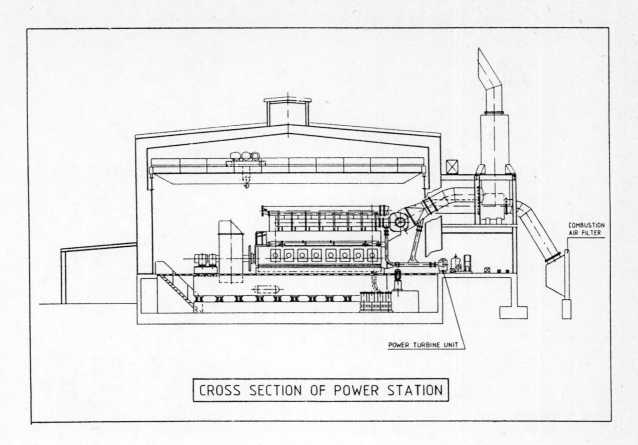

CROSS SECTION OF POWER STATION

COMBUSTION AIR FILTER

POWER TURBINE UNIT

Fig 1

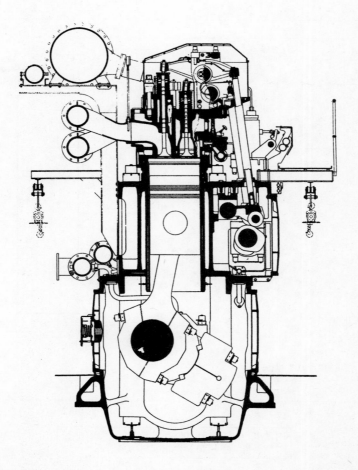

Fig 2

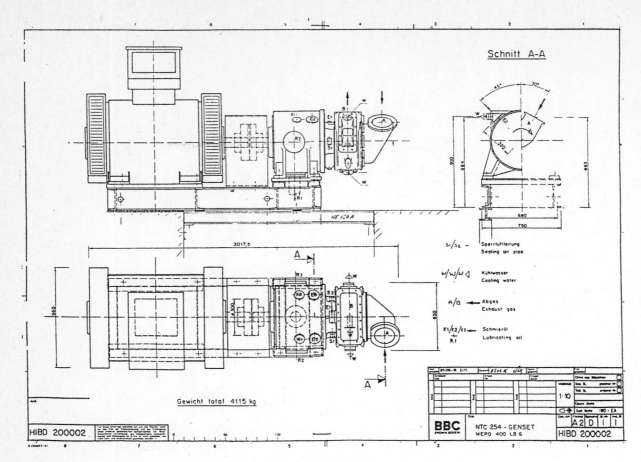

Fig 3   Exhaust gas turbine generator set

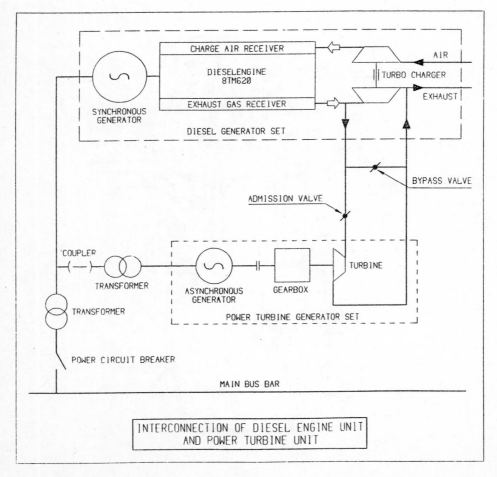

Fig 4

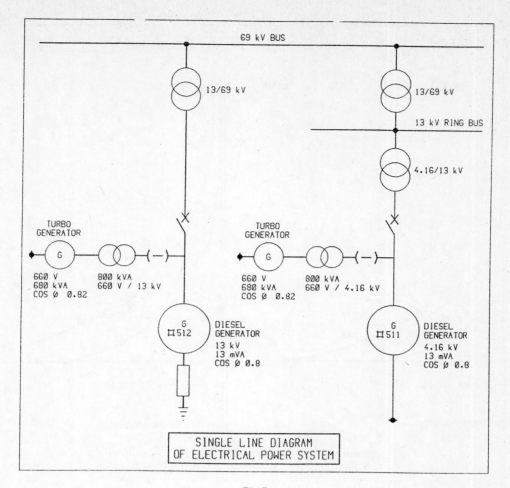

Fig 5

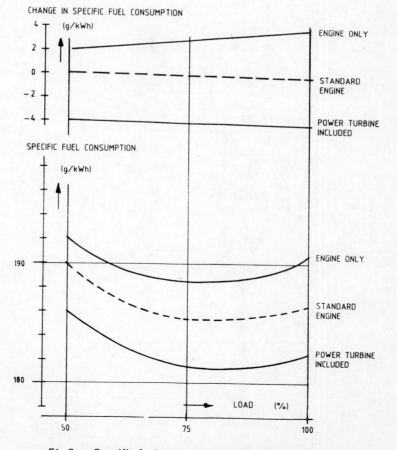

Fig 6   Specific fuel consumption of standard engine and
of engine/power turbine combination

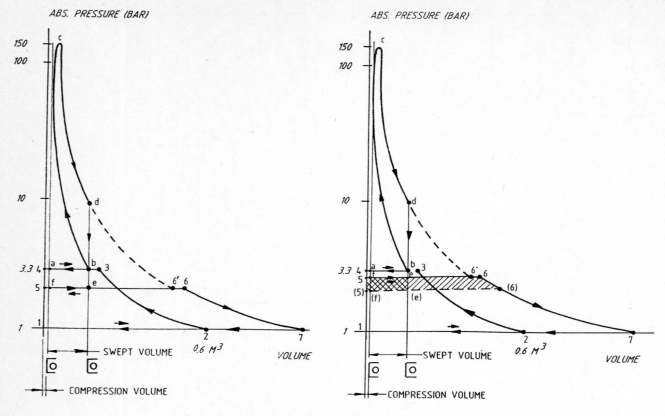

Fig 7   Pressure volume diagram of engine and turbocharger without power turbine (left) and with power turbine (right)

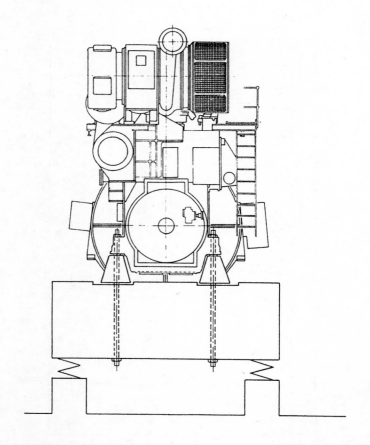

Fig 8

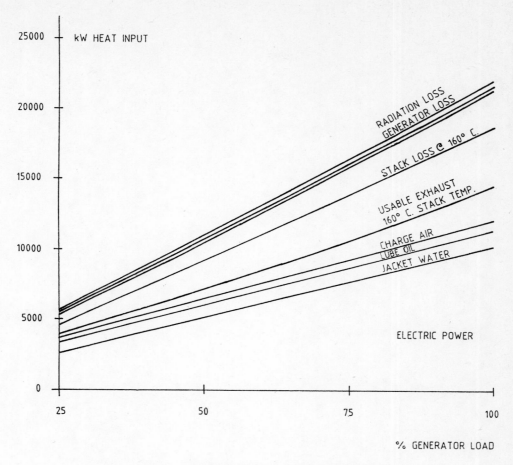

Fig 9   Heat flow distribution in engine 8TM620 (10 600 kW
shaft MCR power at 400 r/min)

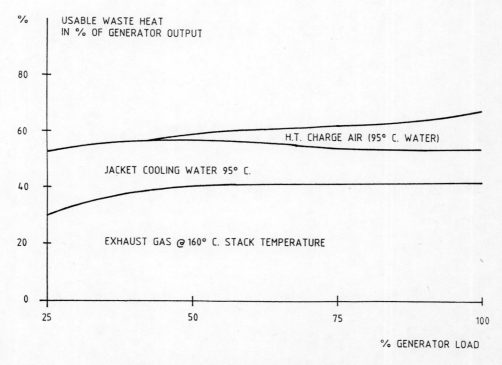

Fig 10   Usable waste heat in percent of generator output as
a function of generator load

Re-equipping North of Scotland Hydro-Electric Board's mobile diesel generator fleet

J A H FORD, CEng, FIMechE, FBIM, FRSA, MIDGTE
Generation Engineer—Diesel, North of Scotland Hydro-Electric Board
H B MACDONALD, CEng, MIMechE
Principal Engineer, North of Scotland Hydro-Electric Board
W BLACK
Operations Director, Aggreko Generators Limited

Synopsis

There are some 23 islands to the north and west of the Scottish mainland which do not have a permanent Power Station and are only supplied with electricity by marine cable. In the event of a marine cable failure the Mobile Diesel Generators are despatched to the island to restore the supply as quickly as possible. The Mobile Diesel Generator fleet in service in the 70's proved to be inadequate, and the paper describes the consultations within the Hydroboard, the co-operation with the manufacturer, Aggreko Generators Limited, and the initial success in supplying the Island of Barra with electricity after a cable failure in May 1988 until reconnected by a new marine cable.

The geography of the North of Scotland comprises a multitude of islands of varying size and the provision and maintenance of electrical power to such areas has, and always will, pose special problems.

In 1948 with the nationalisation of the electrical supply industry, the North of Scotland Hydro-Elecric Board (originally formed in 1942 as a Generating Board) assumed responsibility for transmission and distribution in addition to power generation. The area of supply included, as well as the Scottish mainland, all off-lying islands and the major island groups of the Western Isles, Orkney Isles and Shetland Isles. This distribution area included many small islands to which power supplies were eventually made by submarine cable. In general terms where the maximum demand of an island situation exceeds 3 MVA (approximately), and where the remoteness of the island is not excessive the Board has endeavoured to provide duplicate cables.

There are a considerable number of islands which are only connected to the system with a single submarine cable and it is these particular islands that pose operating problems to the Board in the event of failure. It is against such potential failures that the Board maintains a pool of mobile diesel plant.

While this paper is not essentially on the operation of submarine cables, it is fair to say that the present failure rate is not unreasonable. Statistically it is currently averaged at two failures per annum. The total installed length of

submarine cable is some 316 km and the longest cable in service is 20 km. Failure rate in the early 1970's was high in relation to the total installation, but considerable improvement has now been made in cable design and laying technology.

However, failures do occur. The repair of submarine cables under emergency conditions is, or can be, a lengthy operation dependant on the circumstances. It may involve the use of ships, specially fitted out to raise and handle cables and such ships may not be readily available. As the majority of cable routes are in exposed conditions, repair may be dependent on weather windows. Delays of three/six months are not unknown. Over such periods it is necessary to provide alternative arrangements to ensure a reasonably secure supply. The temporary running of a light interrupter type cable is one method that can be used, if the run is not long or deep and no excessive tidal currents be experienced particularly across the cable.

There are a considerable number of islands within the Board's area where in the event of their supply cable failing, the only way of maintaining the supply until the cable is repaired is by means of temporary generating plant. It is essential that the mobile plant is maintained in readiness, although it is available for other work such as providing supply during essential maintenance. The islands at risk are spread over the Western seaboard of Scotland and throughout the Orkney and Shetland Isles. The maximum demands on these islands vary from 30 kW to 2.5 MW. There is little industrial load on any of the islands and generally the demand is of a domestic nature, the load factor experienced being of the order of 50 – 60%. The method of temporary reconnection under failure conditions has been agreed, and details of the number of consumers and the maximum demand of the various islands is updated on an annual basis. It has been the Board's policy to prepare island sites for temporary generation on islands, and while this work is not yet complete it is proceeding as resources permit.

EMERGENCY PLANT

The concept of the retention of generation plant for emergency purposes by the Hydro-Electric Board is not new and the first units obtained for this purpose were purchased in 1968. The set ratings employed were 410 kW and 200 kW but these sets were difficient in certain aspects. They were skid mounted, canopied sets and were difficult to handle. They also suffered from the vagaries of the climate in a rather harsh environment, not only in operation but under storage conditions which was a necessity outdoors. At the time of purchase there were however severe weight and dimensional restrictions on the handling capacity of the transport facilities that existed throughout the islands.

As the original sets had become run down it was decided to buy a new fleet of generators with a purchase programme phased over several years and to write off the original equipment. Prior to the issuing of enquiries the following main parameters were given consideration.

Rating - In view of the diversity of island load to be supplied by these sets it was considered that the rating of the replacement sets should approximate to that of the original sets, and the set sizes were established at 250 kW and 500 kW.

While the highest load to be supplied was 2.5 MW the average is of the order of 1 -1.5 MW. The night load in many areas is normally of a low order although "offpeak" supplies also pose special problems in most areas.

Prime Mover - The application of small gas turbine units was considered; the major attraction being the weight reduction that would have been achieved with consequent increase in mobility. However, a disadvantage was the logistics of fuel supply to the remote area involved particularly if the requirement was prolonged. It was considered that diesels would be easier to maintain and operate, requiring less specialist knowledge and give better availability under field conditions.

Generation Voltage - The normal distribution primary voltage of the areas to be serviced by the sets is 11 kV, and in order to facilitate connection to these systems it was necessary that the set arrangement could produce power at 11kV. Having the sets wound at 11kV was considered but was abandoned in favour of winding the sets at 415v and employing a separate 415v/11kV step-up transformer on the grounds of cost, standardisation, security and convenience. Overall cost would be increased by 5-10% and an 11kV machine of this size would not be standard. Security in that a generator at 11kV in a set of this size and speed might be vulnerable, whereas a transformer is static and generally robust; convenient in that an 11kV generator created operational difficulties. Winding at the more conventional voltage of 3.3kV for sets in the 500 kW range was obviously not practical in that not only would a transformer to 11kV be required by 415/240 volts would also be required for auxiliary power.

Enclosure - experience with the simple canopy type of enclosure normally employed for small mobile units and used on the previous sets clearly demonstrated the need for a more sophisticated type of enclosure. The difficulties of obtaining complete weather protection and carrying out maintenance with this type of canopy had shown particularly in severe weather, the value of a walk-in type of enclosure. Accordingly it was proposed that standard ISO containers be used as a basis for the containment of the generating sets as this would provide a better environment for on-site operation and maintenance in a hostile climate than previously available from a simple canopied type of unit. At present it is necessary to store the sets in the open, and as periods of storage can be lengthy, a container enclosure, if heated and dehumidified, provides better storage conditions. Ro Ro ferries are now in general use throughout the islands and the additional size and weight of containerisation can be accommodated. It was therefore proposed that the sets be carried on standard fifth wheel coupling trailers. Originally it was intended that the generator enclosure be demountable from the trailer, but due to Road Traffic Regulations this has had to be abandoned and the container is now permanently secured to the trailer. Fifth wheel coupling was chosen as tractors of this type can be readily hired. It was not proposed to purchase tractors.

Ventilation - A major item was that of the radiator cooling system and air flow through the unit. Again, previous experience had highlighted the problems of passing the total cooling air in a salt air environment through the enclosure, as had been done with the original canopy sets. These problems had manifested themselves in contamination of the generator windings, wiring and cabling, failure of relays and control equipment for environmental reasons and corrosion of ferrous materials. It was therefore proposed to specify a system whereby the radiator cooling air bypassed the generator enclosure, the enclosure being ventilated only with sufficient air to dissipate the heat losses from the generating set.

These two latter provisions, set installation within an enclosure providing a walk-in facility and a design affording in effect a separate compartment to house a motor driven fan cooled radiator represents a fairly high increase in capital cost when compared with a more traditional arrangement having a conventional shaft driven fan cooled radiator and close fitting canopy. It is intended however that a life of 25 years be obtained from these sets and although it is not possible to justify such an arrangement on economic grounds this arrangement is considered to be technically superior and operationally desirable.

Batteries - The operational/storage conditions of the original sets had caused considerable difficulties with the battery installation, the batteries being of the lead acid automotive type. In order to overcome these difficulties it was proposed to adopt a more sophisticated approach and to use nickel cadmium batteries and to separate the starting and control functions.

On Board Fuel - As the sets were being provided for a use that would require the setting up of a fuel delivery system it was decided to limit the on-board storage to a nominal amount and a period of 6 hours full load operation was accepted. At the load factors normally experienced this would give an extended period of operation. While the all up weight of the unit was not critical, excessive fuel storage might give movement difficulties and create design problems. As during the design stage it proved feasible to incorporate the same size tank in the 250 kw module, this was agreed.

Having decided the basic parameters of the units, a functional type specification was produced and circulated to all potential operators of the sets, who were invited to comment on the specification. A tender specification was then produced on the basis of the comment received.

The Building of the Generators

Companies were invited to tender for the two types of generator trailer, with a user-specification which set out the reasons for the need and the technical requirements as it saw them. As already explained, the NOSHEB had a very firm idea of what it wanted, based upon considerable operating experience. The successful tenderer was able to recognise the implications of the duty and the operating environment from experience on remote construction sites and on hostile offshore locations.

The target for the design and production team was to achieve two generator vehicles capable of rapid deployment with all necessary operational features and equipment "on board". They were also to be sufficiently durable to survive repeated use under severe conditions and capable of dependable starting and service which would satisfy the Board's standards. In essence the vehicles each comprised a seven tonne capacity swan-neck trailer with fifth wheel coupling; a container generator plant room on the lower deck, and a transformer (supplied by the Board) on the upper deck. A towing vehicle (cab) was not deemed necessary as these are readily available for hire, so the trailers were equipped with jacks for when the generators are in use.

The proposed containerised generator in usual fleet form has a number of fundamental features derived specifically from the demands made by the operator and the environment:

1. To survive on location (and under a hire contract) down-time is a problem and a cost.... a call-out to repair it is time consuming and defeats the purpose of the exercise and involves the supplier in even more costs. The concept of higher specification portable generators for fleet duty considerably reduces the risk of these failures.

2. A "container" must mean just that, if it is to be transported and operated easily, but few manufacturers build everything within the confines of the container housing. "Loose" items often become separated and can be left behind or damaged in an emergency. Similarly, protruding equipment can be damaged and frustrate transportation.

3. Experience has long since proved that "weather protecting" enclosures fabricated from sheet steel lack durability, do not allow walk-in maintenance, and they demand a 100% air flow across the engine and alternator.

4. If the generator room/compartment is to remain comfortable to work in, it must not suffer the full effect of the airflow and the inevitable airborne abrasives etc.. The unusual – if not unique – method of engineering a cooling system satisfied this need.

The last of these design features, the cooling system, is particularly interesting for containerised generators. As can be seen from the illustration, the cooling of the radiator is in a separate compartment, with the fan usually having a vertical axis and being mounted just inside the roof. This effectively leaves just a modest airflow for lateral engine cooling, alternator cooling and aspiration – all of which is filtered and attenuated, aspiration air being drawn directly from outside the container through filters. The exhaust system passes through a duct between the engine compartment and the radiator compartment, and venting to atmosphere well clear of any operator's doors.

Two sizes of generator were built: 500kW and 250kW. The specification components list and even the engines if possible were requested to be either "the same" or "with as many common parts as possible".

The trailer was the same (20 tonne gross) unit for each rating; instrumentation was the same; the containers had only minor differences to accommodate the airflow and exhaust fittings, and the two engines were from the same factory.

It would have been possible to carry this exercise in matching of spare parts to the point where the larger engine was a 12V-form version of a 6-in-line engine but the specified ratings pointed to more cost effective units at the two particular figures. Engineers had considered both of these aspects from experience before making the selection; based on the experience gained through having equipment (particularly engines) in regular daily use.

Both alternators are from the one factory thus continuing the theme of common sourcing. Although in fact, a modern brushless machine requires little if any maintenance and very few spare parts. The alternator rating has been generously selected (625kVA for the 500 kW generator, and 350kVA for the 250 kW generator) to soften the effect of any transient load variations – typically motor starting. The direct engine-alternator coupling by means of a spiggoted and machined ring (matching the flywheel housing) together with a flexible disc drive (to eliminate any torsional vibrational effects) achieves an inherently reliable generator assembly.

The quality of supply is an important feature. The diesel engines use electronic governor controls to achieve A1 regulation to BS.5514 (ISO.3046) thus establishing a 1% (half a cycle) steady state maximum deviation. While the frequency regulation can sometimes present problems (due to the finite and relatively modest power output of a generator compared with a grid supply), modern solid state voltage regulators invariably manage to match or improve upon the national system in most situations, and the comfortably sized alternator ratings already mentioned ease the effect of transient loads. For these generators the AVRs are mounted in the control panel.

Having looked at the "container plant room", the engine-alternator assembly and the electrical supply thus achieved, the control and instrumentation was the next stage. The various services on-board demanded a variety of cabling, all of which was segregated by voltage and numbered for identification:-

* A 415 volt 3 phase 50 hz main generation supply from the generator switched at 415 volts through an air circuit breaker operated by a motor wound spring charged release mechanism. An emergency manual spring charging system is also provided. This out going supply is stepped up to the normal distribution voltage of 11 kV by the on-board transformer auxiliary, 415 and 240 volt supplies are controlled through a three position switch connecting either the main generator supply, the external supply or an emergency generator to A T P + M distribution fuse board.

* 110 volt supply for hand lamps and small tools achieved by a 240/110/25V transformer.

* Battery driven six-hour emergency DC lighting and general engine electrics.

* Secondary charger supply.

All the container wiring is in heavy duty galvanised conduit, and a port in the container provides for an outside supply to be connected.

A free standing control cubicle houses instrumentation of a quality and range selected to ensure a dependable and realistic assessment of operating conditions (ESI standard 50-18). Like all major components, all items had to be common to both vehicles and the major instruments fitted were 98mm scale hermetically sealed. In addition to the voltage, current, frequency, load and power factor instruments, the lub oil pressure and temperature coolant temperature, exhaust temperature and engine speed are also monitored - sufficient information to give warning of any problems and to provide helpful diagnostic evidence.

Paralleling equipment has been incorporated for both sizes of sets to allow either multiple generator service or no-break take-over/disconnection from the mains supply for predictable repair work (e.g. transformer or cable repair or replacement). Synchronising is achieved by simple manual controls, but a "check synchronising" circuit is fitted which disallows incorrect use.

Starting, the most obviously vital and yet the most easily overlooked function, is the subject of seemingly excessive precautions. As this aspect of the generator has proved to be the most prone to failure, it was to be matched by duplicated systems. There is the normal battery driven motor starting with a charger complete with its own "Earth Fault" and "Supply failure" alarms.

To back this up a small self-contained generator, driven by an air-cooled diesel delivers a 7.0kW single phase 240V supply. Being hand-start, this generator effectively provides something akin to a black-start ability. As has already been mentioned, the vehicle is wired to cater for a secondary charger supply utilising the 240/110/25V transformer. Thus two methods of battery charging are provided, and these facilities plus the regular planned maintenance programme avoid the common problems associated with starting temporary mobile plant.

On-board fuel storage for more than six hours at full load was specified, and the tank positioned below the cooling (fan) plenum chamber more than satisfies this need. In addition to the prismatic sight glass contents guage (which is inherently maintenance free and reliable) a four contact level switch provides "Low" and "High" level warnings and start and stop controls for the electric fuel transfer pump. The permanent fuel line is in stainless steel, and a 10m coupling hose complete with terminations are housed on-board. Just for good measure, a hand operated fuel transfer pump is fitted.

These vehicles are called into service at short notice and often in difficult and remote circumstances. The operating engineers must have as many services at their disposal as is practical. It has already been established that the fan cooling system effectively reduces the generator room conditions to a gentle filtered airflow. The exhaust silencer and pipework is lagged and clad in aluminium; tools and spares are stowed on-board - as are a set of manuals and a plastic sealed and mounted diagram. There are two fire protection systems; one being an automatically sensed and manually released halon gas installation (controllable from outside) and the other being three strategically positioned dry powder extinguishers.

The overall paint protection finish was also of prime importance to Aggreko. After gritblasting the paint finish was zinc rich primer, followed by two coats of 2 pack epoxy enamel.

SOUTH UIST TO ERISKAY MARINE CABLE FAILURE

At 2003 hours on Thursday, 7 May 1987, the electricity supply was lost to the islands of Eriskay, Barra and Vatersay which are the three most southerly islands of the Outer Hebridean chain of islands. These three islands with a demand of about 1.5/2.0 Megawatts are one of the major risks to be covered by the Mobile Diesel Generator Fleet. After the initial investigation to find the cause of the loss of supply, at 0050 hours on Friday, 8 May, it was reported that the marine cable between the islands of South Uist and Eriskay had failed and mobile diesel generators were requested on either Barra or Eriskay to restore the supply.

The first step in organising a response is usually to charter a ship to transport the bulk of the equipment to the island from wherever it happens to be located at the time. After the initial response, additional equipment can usually be despatched on regular sailings as the shipping companies will make space available to deal with an emergency situation.

While immediate arrangements to charter a vessel could not be made, work on load-testing the generators began immediately. Past experience has shown that testing of a mobile diesel generator by just proving that it will start is just not good enough. Test facilities for running the mobile diesel generators on load have already been installed at the Oban Depot and at Loch Carnan Power Station. Similar test facilities are planned for Lerwick Power Station.

By mid-morning of 8th May it was established that the MV Claymore (1,640 tons) was en route to Oban and could be taken on charter from 1600 hours.

At the time of the incident 2 x 250 MDGs were located in Oban and 2 x 500kW and 1 x 250kW were located at Loch Carnan Power Station, South Uist. Generators were loaded at Oban and at Lochboisdale, South Uist, and then the ferry sailed to Castlebay on the island of Barra. As the old fleet of diesel generators was skid-mounted, This was the first occasion in which the response could be planned without cranage being provided at every movement point and shipping out a mobile crane for usage at the site of the emergency power station. This was a major step forward.

A pool of experienced operators exists within the Diesel Group and additional staff are always trained during each incident. A Senior Engineer from each location attended the acceptance tests at the manufacturer's factory to familiarise himself with the new MDG's to enable him in turn to instruct his staff.

During the Friday morning and early afternoon, the diesel generators were tested at Oban and Loch Carnan and prepared for shipping. Also, arrangements had been made to purchase diesel fuel from the tanks at the local fish meal factory.

Prior to the MV Claymore leaving Oban there was an urgent request from the fish factory on Barra for a refrigeration container to be taken to Barra to save the bulk of the fish held in cold storage from going rotten. The MV Claymore sailed to Lochboisdale, collected the remainder of the MDGs and subsequently arrived at Castlebay at 0400 hours on Saturday, 9 May. At 1235 hours the first consumers were reconnected and all the consumers on Barra and Vatersay were connected by 1614 hours. Supply was returned on Eriskay at 2025 hours. Shortly after the ship berthed, most of the fish in the island's cold store was saved by being transferred to the refrigerator container. Communications are all important in this type of exercise and the NOSHEB had an excellent response from British Telecom who installed a telephone on the Saturday just as soon as the emergency power station was established.

Simultaneously with the establishment of an emergency power station on Barra, attempts were being made to run a temporary replacement cable link comprising three sections of polymeric interrupter cable. Unfortunately this temporary cable failed under pressure test but subsequently was commissioned at 2230 hours on 13 May and remained in service until a new cable was provided.

The MDGs then ran for a four day period whilst the changeover was carried out. The new cable was commissioned on Wednesday, 1 June 1988, and the MDGs and other equipment were removed from the Island of Barra on the regular ferry sailings.

CONCLUSIONS

The re-equipping of the mobile diesel generator fleet gave the Hydro Board the opportunity to re-appraise the unique operating problems associated with the emergency supply of the islands, to take advantage of the improvements in the island transport facilities and to incorporate the latest and best practices offered by the manufacturer.

The easing of the weight restrictions allowed for a containerised unit and transformer to be mounted permanently on a trailer. Not having to find cranes for each move, and the avoidance of making LV connections on site have been a great benefit. The fact that all the staff involved in these operations were given the opportunity to comment before the specification was finalised added some practical improvements, not to mention an improvement in staff morale. An integral part of this project was the provision of on-load test facilities and the importance of this provision cannot be over-emphasized.

In the design and manufacture of the generator vehicles the supplier drew on its wide experience of supplying units to cope with the hazardous conditions encountered in the North Sea Oil Industry, and co-operated in incorporating the special features specified by the Hydro Board. A combination of all these facets led to the initial success in supplying the island of Barra subsequent to the Uist/Eriskay marine cable failure in May 1988. This has been followed by a similar good performance in supplying the small island of Berneray.

ACKNOWLEDGMENTS

The authors wish to express their thanks to the North of Scotland Hydro-Electric Board and Aggreko Generators Limited for permission to publish the information contained in this paper. The opinions expressed, however, are attributable solely to the authors. The authors would like to thank their colleagues in their respective organisations who have assisted with the preparation of this paper.

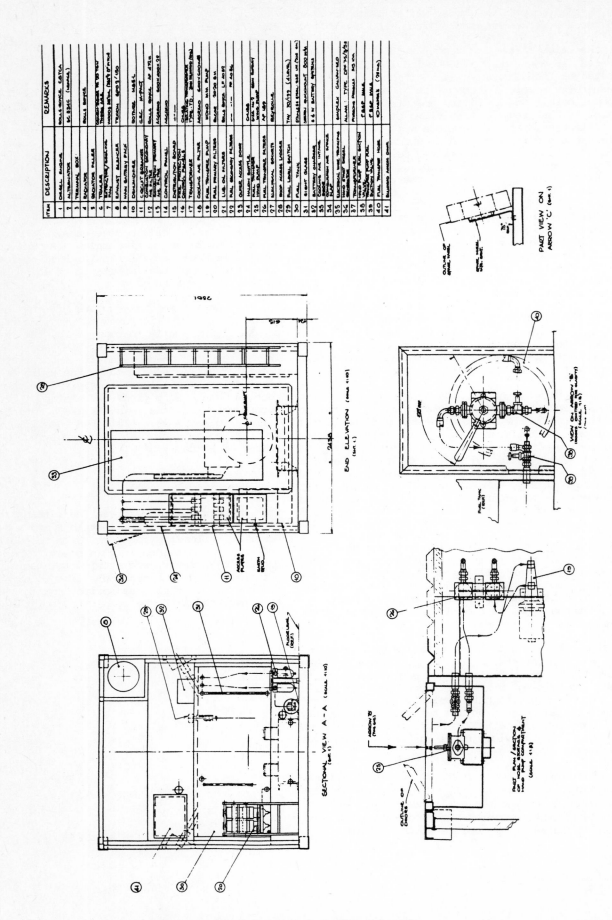

Fig 4   Mobile generator — general arrangement

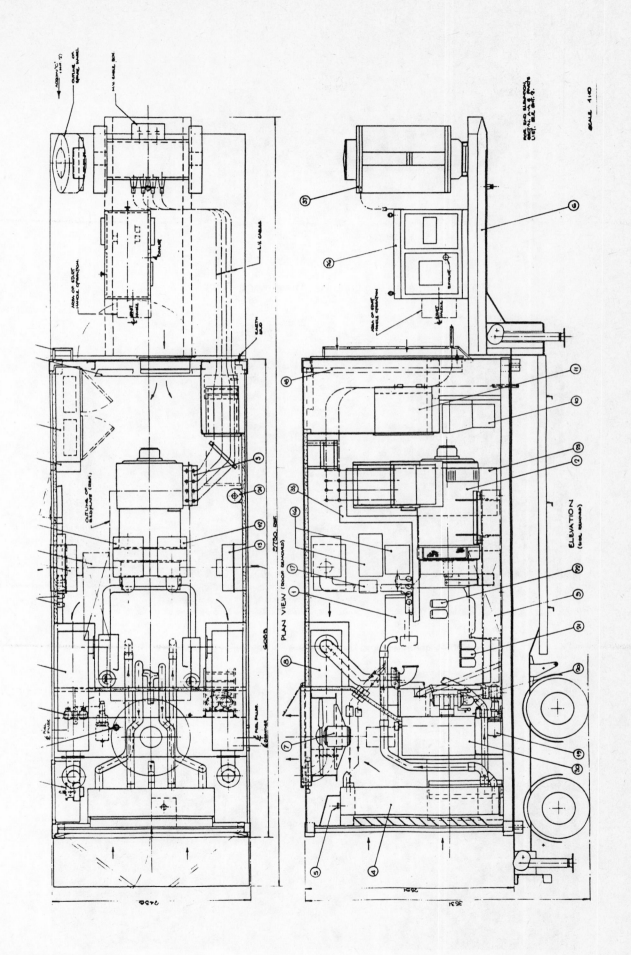

79

Fig 1   A cutaway of a typical containerised generator

Fig 2   500kW generator and transformer awaiting delivery to the Hydro Board

Fig 3   Mobile diesel generators at the Hydro Board's Oban depot connected
to the full load test facilities

The practical applications of modern monitoring techniques to a diesel power station

F A RICHARDS, BSc, CEng, MIMarE
Deputy Power Station Manager, States of Guernsey Electricity Board
A T WOODFORD, BTech, AMIMechE
Assistant Production Engineer, States of Guernsey Electricity Board

SYNOPSIS

The paper examines the application of some modern monitoring techniques to a Power Station using slow-speed and medium-speed diesel engines as prime movers. The paper is intended as a "user's view" of the merits and cost-effectiveness of such techniques. Since the Power Station in question represents the sole generating capacity of the community, the requirement for reliability of plant is paramount, and possible conflicts between reliability and cost effectiveness are examined, but examples of real cost savings are also demonstrated.

1. INTRODUCTION

The States of Guernsey Electricity Board (SEB) is the publicly owned utility responsible for the generation and distribution of electricity in the Channel Island of Guernsey. It currently meets a maximum demand of 55 MWe from its 25300 consumers utilising diesel generators running on heavy fuel oil.

The plant in use comprises -

```
1 off Sulzer 9RTA 58    14.2 MWe
3 off Sulzer 9RNF 68    12.2 MWe
6 off Mirrlees KVM12      3.5 MWe
```

A fundamental requirement of an island power station, with no national grid to fall back on, is one of reliability. It is this need for reliability which has a significant influence on the maintenance and monitoring techniques used by the SEB.

Additionally, with the purchase of some 45,000 tonnes of fuel each year, this being the highest single cost to the organisation, optimum utilisation of fuel is essential.

This paper aims to show how recent developments in monitoring techniques can increase the efficiency of the day-to-day operation of diesel engines in an electricity generation environment.

2. PERFORMANCE MONITORING OF SLOW-SPEED DIESEL PLANT

For many years, efficiency of generating plant has been considered an important factor in the operation of the SEB. Initially, this simply meant that availability and usage of the most efficient plant was maximised, but more recently a number of important routines have been developed.

When the Sulzer 2-stoke engines were commissioned (1979 onwards), individual engine fuel metering allowed the daily efficiency of each engine to be accurately calculated. At first, the efficiency was measured in terms of kWh per litre of fuel, and later the Specific Fuel Consumption in g/kWh. Plotting graphs of these parameters on a daily basis is the first real step towards active efficiency control, in that it enables staff to identify falling efficiency and to monitor the effect of any remedial action.

The next significant advance was the installation of real-time efficiency display for the C-Station engines in 1983. These instruments are mounted in the Central Control Room, and display kWh per litre of fuel, updated every 20 seconds. These have been found invaluable for rapid identification of problems, and also introduced a degree of cost awareness to the Operations staff.

In 1984, the existing C-Station engines were fitted with a package of efficiency improvement modifications, which primarily consisted of uprated fuel pumps and the Sulzer "Fuel Quality Setting" mechanism (FQS). The FQS is particularly important in the context of this paper in that it allows fuel injection timing to be easily adjusted whilst the engine is running. The significance of this will become apparent later.

Maximum benefit of the FQS can only be obtained if the combustion pressure within the engine can be accurately measured. At this time, it was not felt that the mechanical peak pressure indicator was sufficiently accurate for this purpose, and alternatives were sought. In 1985 the Autronica NK-5 system was installed, which has since become a major influence on our performance monitoring programme.

2.1 The Autronica NK-5 System

Each of the four C-Station engines is fitted with the following equipment:

1 x Combustion Pressure Transducer
1 x Fuel Injection Pressure Transducer
1 x Scavenge Air Pressure Transducer
1 x Speed/Crankshaft Position Sensor

Although it is possible to have dedicated Combustion and Injection pressure transducers for each cylinder on all engines this was not felt to be cost effective. Furthermore, the use of portable transducers for each engine provides the additional benefit of greater repeatability between cylinders.

The sensors for all engines are connected to a Central Processing Unit which includes CRT display, data storage facilities and a graphics printer. A schematic diagram of the complete system is shown in fig 1.

The system is capable of displaying combustion and injection pressure variation through an engine revolution. In addition, specific parameters relating to these curves are calculated and displayed. Example curves are shown for reference in fig 2. The curves and associated data can be stored on floppy disk for future reference, and the numerical data can be stored in internal memory until overwritten by new data.

2.2 Operation of the System

It is normally the practice to monitor the engines with this equipment under the following circumstances:

1. When the station HFO supply tank is changed, especially if there is a significant difference in the analysis of the fuels.

2. Following any significant maintenance or adjustments to the engines.

3. If there is reason to suspect the combustion or injection processes (eg. falling efficiency, suspicion of misfiring, etc.)

4. In the absence of any of the above, it is considered preferable to check engines at least every two weeks.

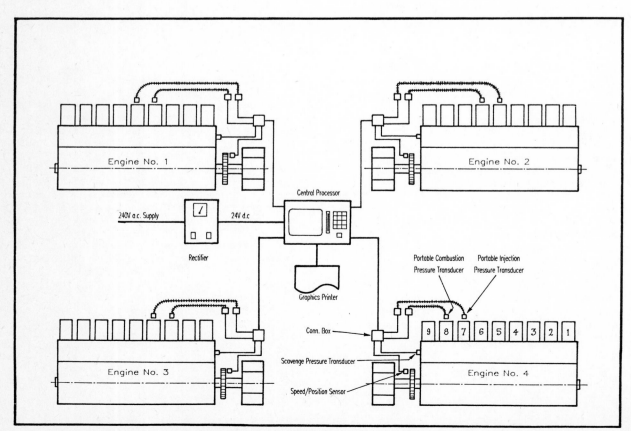

Fig 1   Schematic diagram of Autronica NK-5 system

The equipment may be operated by any reasonably competent staff, but analysis of results is normally the responsibility of engineering staff.

Fig 2(a)   Example of combustion pressure curve

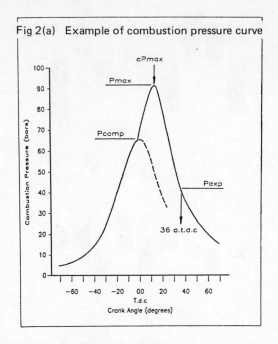

Fig 2(b)   Example of injection pressure curve

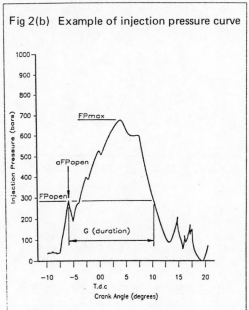

2.3   Benefits of Routine Performance Monitoring

We have identified three specific areas in which regular monitoring with this equipment can be advantageous. These are as follows:

2.3.1   Short Term Efficiency Optimisation

The base load engines operate predominantly on Heavy (Residual) Fuel Oil, which although bought from one supplier may originate from many sources worldwide. The composition of the fuel, and subsequent engine performance, can therefore vary considerably.

It is our experience that significant cost savings can be made by adjustment of injection timing such that the peak combustion pressure (Pmax) is maintained as close as possible to the manufacturers recommended values. This can be easily achieved using the FQS mechanism. We have found that the effect of such adjustments is a reduction in specific fuel consumption of about 1 g/kWh for each degree of advance of injection timing. Whilst this may seem fairly insignificant at first sight, this can add up to substantial savings when, as in our case, base load plant is operating with 1 or 2 degrees advance for long periods of time. An example of the combustion pressure curves before and after FQS adjustment, together with the effect of that adjustment on Specific Fuel Consumption is shown in Fig 3.

Fig 3   Effect of a 2 degree advance of injection timing
Engine C3, 9RNF-68M

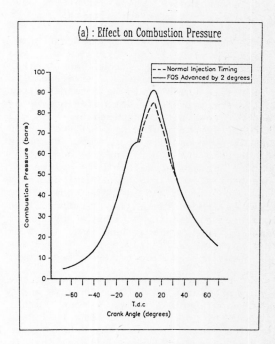

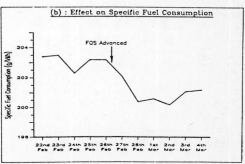

Although cost savings are difficult to quantify, we are convinced that the installation costs of the equipment have been more than recovered in the relatively short period of use. With the SEB using some 45,000 tonnes of HFO per year, a reduction of only 1% makes this a worthwhile investment, even at today's low fuel prices. It must be noted however, that these savings could not be achieved without the facility to adjust injection timing easily and whilst the engine is running.

2.3.2 Long Term Efficiency Optimisation

In the longer term, it is our aim to improve and maintain the engine efficiency as high as possible. To this end, we seek to minimise performance variations between cylinders by adjustment to fuel pump actuation cams and compression shim thickness.

Great care is taken to ensure that such adjustments are made on the basis of consistent measurements over a period of time, rather than "one-off" readings, consequently we are still in the process of adjusting some engines to our satisfaction. We can however report two specific instances where benefits have been gained from such adjustments:

i) On our No. 3 engine, the peak combustion pressure on Cylinder 7 was consistently higher than any other cylinder on that engine. As a result, the benefits which could be obtained from short term efficiency optimisation using the FQS were always limited by that one cylinder in particular. The fuel pump actuation cam on this engine was retarded by 1 degree, thus bringing the combustion pressure into line with other cylinders. Consequently, the FQS adjustment could be made on the basis of the combustion pressures across the engine, rather than being restricted by a single cylinder. This, in some cases, has resulted in an extra degree of advance, with the subsequent fuel saving as described above.

ii) On our No. 2 engine, the peak combustion pressures on Cylinders 1, 4 and 9 were consistently lower than other cylinders by up to 2 bars. The fuel pump actuation cams for these cylinders were each advanced by 1 degree, resulting in improved balance in combustion pressures for that engine. In addition, a reduction in specific fuel consumption of about 1 g/kWh was noted. These effects are demonstrated in Fig 4.

Whilst the improvements in engine efficiency as a result of such adjustments are relatively small, the total savings when carried forward over the lifetime of the engine are substantial.

An additional benefit of both long and short term efficiency optimisation is that the overall condition of the engines is arguably improved. Although this is

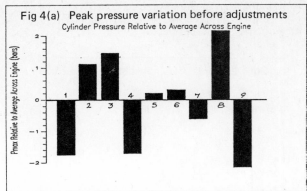

Fig 4(a) Peak pressure variation before adjustments
Cylinder Pressure Relative to Average Across Engine

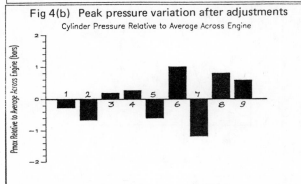

Fig 4(b) Peak pressure variation after adjustments
Cylinder Pressure Relative to Average Across Engine

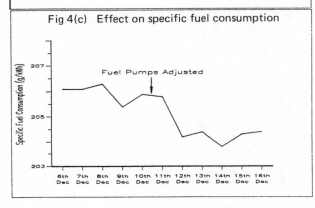

Fig 4(c) Effect on specific fuel consumption

impossible to quantify, it has been noticed for example that the scavenge and piston underside spaces are cleaner.

2.3.3 Maintenance Decision Making Aid

The analysis of results can provide useful assistance in the planning of maintenance and repairs to the engines, in particular the fuel injection system. Traditionally fuel injectors have been replaced and reconditioned every 1500 engine running hours, but now this period is shortened or extended to suit actual performance.

There are also numerous instances where this equipment has been instrumental in the identification of faults on the engines which would otherwise have been difficult and time consuming to isolate. Examples of these are as follows:

i) Identification of individual blocked injectors, causing partial misfire on one cylinder of an engine. In these instances, the injection pressure tends to be noticably higher than normal, whilst the combustion pressure is lower. In the example shown in fig 5, the cause was found to be small particles of welding "spatter" blocking the injector nozzle holes. Since this High Pressure fuel pipe had been recently replaced, this was thought to be the most likely source of the problem. It should be noted that it would have been difficult to identify this problem using conventional methods.

ii) At one time, considerable problems were encountered with sets of fuel injectors which had recently been reconditioned by an approved sub-contractor. The symptoms of these problems were that after a few days of being installed on the engines, fuel efficiency began to rapidly fall, and the fuel injection pressures rose, in some cases to a level where there was a danger

of lifting the relief valves. The problem was referred back to the subcontractor several times, and eventually traced to incorrect machining of the injector needles, causing them to seize after a relatively short time. The results obtained using the Autronica equipment were instrumental in identifying this problem.

iii) On one occasion, it was discovered that fuel pumps had been incorrectly calibrated during routine maintenance of the engine. A check with the Autronica equipment immediately identified which fuel pumps required recalibration, as shown in Fig 6. Without such equipment it would have been necessary to check all the fuel pumps, resulting in extra labour costs and a much longer outage of the first merit engine.

Fig 5(a) Effect of blocked injector on combustion pressure

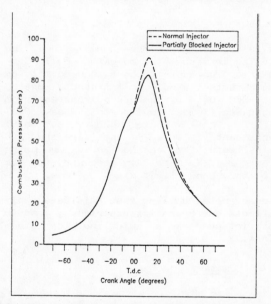

Fig 6(a) Effect of incorrectly calibrated fuel pump on combustion pressure

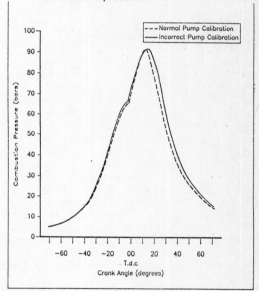

Fig 5(b) Effect of blocked injector on injection pressure

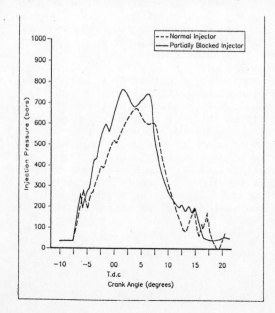

Fig 6(b) Effect of incorrectly calibrated fuel pump on injection pressure

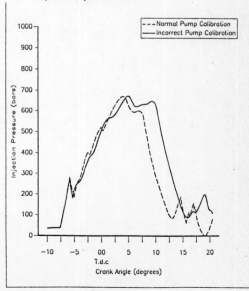

2.4 Correlation of Results with Fuel Oil Properties

For the past few years, some of the major oil companies have devoted extensive research to the properties and behaviour of Heavy Fuel Oils. As a result of these investigations, the concept of "ignitability" of fuels has been developed, and efforts have been made to correlate this concept with physical properties of the fuel. Particular examples of these are the Calculated Carbon Aromaticity Index (CCAI) derived by Shell (1) and the Calculated Ignition Index (CII-1) of BP (2). Whilst a detailed explanation of these properties may be found in the references, in essence research showed that the ignition performance of a Heavy Fuel Oil could be related to the degree of aromaticity of the fuel which was in turn approximated to a function of density and viscosity.

Since then, this property has been related to actual engine performance on several occasions (3) (4). Experience at the SEB can generally confirm the findings of these investigations, and possibly enhance them in the following ways:

i) The CCAI or CII-1 of a fuel can provide an effective ranking of the fuel in terms of ignition quality, and subsequent effects on combustion. Whilst it may be true that slow-speed engines are less prone than are medium-speed to the effects of poor ignition quality, we do have evidence that fuels with a high CCAI (870 or more) can have adverse effects on the operation of slow-speed engines. These effects include rapid rate of combustion pressure rise, higher peak combustion pressures, and increased heat transfer to combustion space components (evident by higher than normal cooling water temperatures). An example of how such a fuel may affect the combustion

pressures is shown in Fig 7, whilst the possible consequences to the engine have been documented in the above references.

ii) It has been stated in the past (4) that fuel with low CCAI (850 or less) will give "normal" engine performance in terms of the likelihood of engine damage as a result of using such fuel. Whilst this may be true, it is our experience that fuels with low CCAI (good ignition quality) tend to cause a different problem, namely that of lower engine effiency, which we combat using the FQS adjustments described in 2.3.1. As an example, consider the case of our first merit engine, and its CCAI related performance as shown in Fig. 8. This may be summarised as follows:

CCAI	Typical FQS Adjustment	Reduction in Sfc
<830	2 deg advance	2 g/kWh approx
830-845	1 deg advance	1 g/kWh approx
845-855	Normal injection Timing	
>855	Variable	

As is apparent from the above, without the FQS adjustments the Specific Fuel Consumption would be greater than normal by the amounts stated. At present, most of the HFO used by the SEB originates from North Sea fields, and normally has a CCAI within the range 820 to 835. Consequently, were it not for the FQS adjustments the engines would be using about 2 g/kWh more than necessary for the time they used this fuel.

Please note however that this data only reflects our operating experience, and is not intended as a guideline for other plant.

2.5 Summary

We believe that efficiency considerations are important for the operation of large diesel plant. The combination of routine efficiency calculation and engine monitoring enables us to successfully optimise plant efficiency under a wide range of circumstances.

The monitoring equipment is also useful for assistance with maintenance decision making. It allows problems to be identified which would otherwise have been difficult and time consuming to trace. We remain firmly of the opinion that the system has more than justified its installation cost, even with the present relatively low price of fuel. Certainly, we intend to use similar systems again on any new base load plant to be installed in the future.

Fig 7   Effect of high CCAI fuel on combustion pressure

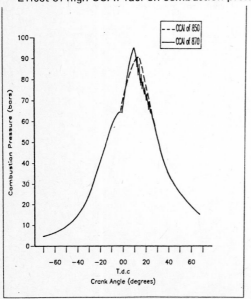

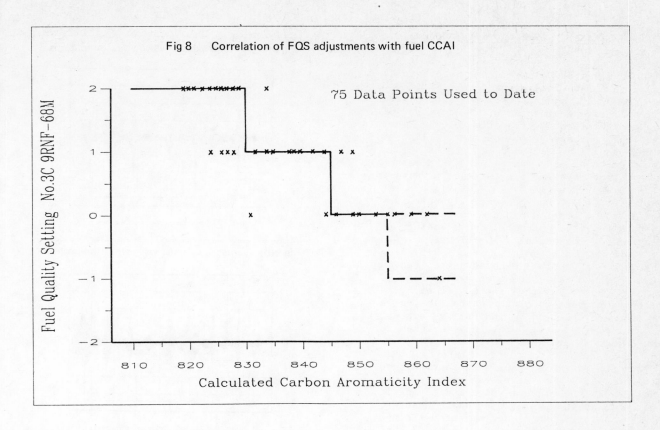

Fig 8   Correlation of FQS adjustments with fuel CCAI

3. **VIBRATION MONITORING APPLICATIONS**

Over the past few years, the subject of vibration monitoring as used for condition based maintenance has received extensive coverage in technical press and seminars. We are aware of many situations where vibration based condition monitoring is used on similar plant to ours, and where operators have claimed a great deal of success.

The situation at the SEB is rather different in that, despite detailed investigations on several occasions in the past, we have so far been unable to justify the use of vibration condition monitoring as a cost effective proposition, except in certain specific cases which are explained later. The reasons for this are as follows:

i) The task of collecting data for analysis tends to be fairly labour intensive, and from cost considerations could only be done by the Engine Room Attendants. These staff, being relatively unskilled, would require easy to operate equipment, which tends to be more expensive than the basic instruments.

ii) In-service failures of equipment are rare, and no instances are recalled where extensive damage to plant has resulted from failure (with the exception of cooling tower fans which are discussed later).

iii) The Power Station is permanently manned, and impending failures are usually noticed by the Shift Charge Engineers by simple observation.

iv) Since all auxiliaries are duplicated (i.e. duty/standby) occasional failures can be tolerated without affecting the operation of the Power Station.

v) The annual load variation requires that main engines are overhauled during the summer months only. Auxiliary plant is maintained at the same time. Therefore to gain any real benefit, we must be satisfied that the interval between maintenance could be extended by a further complete year, since anything less would require plant outages at periods of high load when we could least afford it. So far, we remain unconvinced that this is a practical proposition.

The majority of plant and auxiliaries are maintained based upon an interval of running hours. To assist with this, a computer system is used, which was described in detail by Mr Richards in 1983 (5). Whilst such a system will undoubtedly mean that plant is maintained more frequently than required, the system has proved extremely effective in assisting with maintenance planning and ensuring reliability of plant.

There are certain instances where we have considered vibration monitoring to be effective. These are usually in the cases where failure of plant would have major implications to Power Station operations, and where identification of a potential problem is impossible by "feel". These instances include:

3.1 Exhaust Valves on Medium Speed Engines

The Mirrlees KV Major engines were, until 1979, the base load plant of the SEB. One of the more frequent problems encountered with these engines was the failure of exhaust valves, which often caused more serious damage to pistons, liners, turbochargers, etc. To combat this problem the SEB installed a vibration monitoring system for exhaust valves. This was described in detail by Mr Richards (5), but essentially works by using the vibration pattern caused by the exhaust valve opening and closing to identify potential problems. To illustrate this point, the vibration pattern of a normal exhaust valve, and a badly burned valve are compared in Fig 9. Notice that in the latter case, the vibration pattern of the valve closing is much more "blurred", indicating exhaust gases leaking past. This may be taken as an advanced warning of failure.

Since the Sulzer engines were commissioned the use of the Mirrlees engines has declined, and exhaust valve monitoring is not used as much as it once was. However, for stations running medium speed engines on base load, it is strongly advised that this method be investigated.

3.2 C-Station Cooling Tower Fans

Vibration monitoring was installed on these items at the end of 1987 because of a number of failures encountered during that year (caused by the actual equipment design and not lack of maintenance). The reasons that this is considered a suitable case for vibration monitoring are that the equipment is inaccessible for manual checks, and vital for Power Station operation (there being no redundancy of these units).

Up to now, we have only limited experience of this equipment, and are therefore unable to comment on the effectiveness of such monitoring. However, we have used the results to extend the interval between routine maintenance on several of these units.

3.3 "Fingerprinting" of Main Engines

The routine measurement of vibration levels at various strategic locations around the C-Station engines has been used since the plant was commissioned. Whilst this is done fairly infrequently (roughly every 6 months), it has been useful in establishing an overall "fingerprint" of vibration of these engines. This has proved useful on occasions in the past where modifications have been made to the engines, which have caused increased vibration at certain locations on the engine.

An example of this was when the RNF engines were fitted with the high

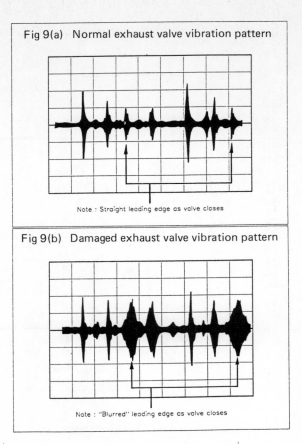

Fig 9(a) Normal exhaust valve vibration pattern

Note : Straight leading edge as valve closes

Fig 9(b) Damaged exhaust valve vibration pattern

Note : "Blurred" leading edge as valve closes

efficiency fuel pumps, which were essentially shorter stroke and larger bore than the original pumps. The consequence of this was a substantial increase in vibration close to the fuel pumps, which was rectified by the installation of large strengthening brackets.

Whilst, in the example above, it was apparent simply by inspection that vibration levels had increased, the use of vibration fingerprinting enabled this increase to be quantified thus providing a more accurate account. of the problem. Furthermore, the effect of remedial modifications could be easily established.

3.4 Summary

The practice of the SEB is to apply vibration monitoring where it is considered essential, or where its cost can be justified. We are aware of significant and rapid developments in this field, and consequently feel that the subject must be periodically reviewed. However, at this present time we feel that we cannot justify the use of widespread vibration monitoring as a basis for condition maintenance.

4. FUEL TREND ANALYSIS

For the past eight years the SEB has carried out laboratory analyses on all fuel deliveries.

The parameters assessed are -

Density @ 15 degrees C.
Flashpoint   degrees C.
Sediment by hot filtration % wt.
Sulphur content % wt.
Viscosity, Kinematic @ 100 degrees C.
Water content % vol.
Toluene equivalence point % vol (TEP)
(tendency to sludge formation).

Derived from these are -

Fuel temperature required to give
12.5 cSt viscosity at injector.

Calculated carbon aromacity index.

Fuel supplier is required to provide -

Ash % wt.
Aluminium ppm (Representing Catalytic
Fines).

Initially, some of this data was used to confirm delivered quantities and stock levels, but latterly it has been more closely related to running behaviour.

As shown in section 2.4, the CCAI figure is used to indicate what adjustments to the injection timing may be required in order to optimise performance.

The use of the predicted temperature for the correct fuel injection viscosity (by extrapolation from the result at 100 degrees C) has proved more effective as a means of achieving accurate fuel injection temperature control than the use of visco-meters. The lifting of fuel pump relief valves is now a rare occurrence.

During the past eight years two deliveries of fuel have been found to be unusable, but only after getting into the station systems and creating serious operating problems.

In one of these instances no individual parameter was outside acceptable limits, but on further examination of the particular combinations of results a clearer picture emerged, as shown in Fig 10.

The particular delivery (Sample No. 252) showed higher than normal levels of -

    Water
    Sulphur
    Sediment
    TEP

This fuel created serious sludging problems in the fuel treatment system.

A later delivery (Sample No. 276) had higher than normal levels of -

    Sulphur
    Sediment
    TEP

This similarity provided a warning that there was a possibility of a repeated problem, so a hold was put on the use of the fuel until further tests were carried out. With the more normal water content level the sludging problem did not re-occur. It was, however, found necessary to switch off the centrifuge water injection system to avoid recreating the problem.

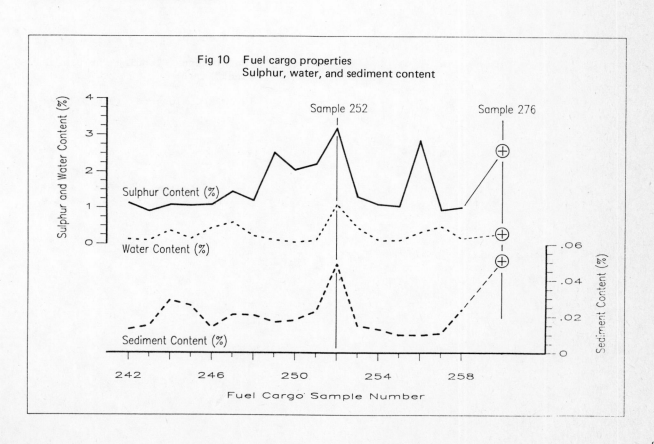

Fig 10   Fuel cargo properties
Sulphur, water, and sediment content

There can be conflicting requirements for the operation of the "Alcap" type Fuel Oil centrifuges now that they are fitted with the water injection (or "sludge conditioning") system. This water injection was found to be necessary to "flush out" dry sludge from the centrifuge bowl when using fuels with a combination of high levels of catalytic fines (or other sediment) and low water content.

Where a fuel has a tendency towards sludge formation (as was the case for Sample No. 252), any additional water injection only exacerbates the problem. Under these circumstances, prior knowledge of the fuel properties enables a view to be taken on how best to operate the fuel treatment system.

5.   CONCLUSIONS

This paper demonstrates that there are real and lasting benefits to be gained by the use of modern monitoring techniques. The methods employed do however need to be selected with care in order to be appropriate to the plant, its mode of operation, and type of staff, and need to be critically examined to ensure that they are reliable and cost effective.

6.   **REFERENCES**

(1)   A P Zeelenberg, H J Fijn van Draat and H L Barker

"The Ignition Performance of Fuel Oils in Marine Diesel Engines"

CIMAC (1983)

(2)   P David and M J Denham

"The Measurement and Prediction of the Ignition Quality of Residual Fuel Oils"

Trans IMarE (TM), Vol 96, Paper 66 (1984)

(3)   D G Richardson, G Armstrong, C N Pontikos, and P S Katsoulakos

"The Analysis of Marine Fuels with Reference to Diesel Engine Perform- ance"

North East Coast Institute of Engineers and Shipbuilders, Trans Vol 103, No 3 (1987)

(4)   H Sjoberg

"Combustion Studies and Endurance Tests on Low Ignition Quality Fuel Oils"

Trans IMarE (TM), Vol 99, Paper 24 (1987)

(5)   F A Richards

"Maintenance Planning for Diesel Plant"

INPOWER Conference (1985), Paper D